REVISE FOR RELIGIOUS STUDIES GCSE

AQA B

Truth, Spirituality and Contemporary Issues

David Worden

heinemann.co.uk
✓ Free online support
✓ Useful weblinks
✓ 24 hour online ordering

01865 888058

Inspiring generations

Heinemann Educational Publishers
Halley Court, Jordan Hill, Oxford OX2 8EJ
Part of Harcourt Education

Heinemann is the registered trademark of
Harcourt Education Limited

© David Worden 2003

First published 2003

08 07
10 9 8 7 6

British Library Cataloguing in Publication Data is available
from the British Library on request.

978 0 435 30701 1

Designed by Artistix
Typeset by TechType, Abingdon, Oxon

Original illustrations © Harcourt Education Limited, 2003

Illustrated by TechType, Abingdon, Oxon
Printed in the UK by CPI Bath
Cover photo © Photodisc

Acknowledgements
The publishers would like to thank the following for the use of copyright material: © UK transplant for
the donor card image on p.17; The National Blood service for the use of the logo on p.17.

The publishers would like to thank the following for the use of photographs:

Alamy p. 33, p. 39, p. 56; Corbis p. 7, p. 49, p. 58; Gareth Boden p. 22; PA photos p. 49; Rose Handy p. 10;
Trevor Clifford p. 40

There are links to relevant web sites in this book. In order to ensure that the links are up-to-date, that
the links work, and that the sites are not inadvertently linked to sites that could be considered offensive,
we have made the links available on the Heinemann website at www.heinemann.co.uk/hotlinks. When
you access the site, the express code is **7010P**.

Every effort has been made to contact copyright holders of material reproduced in this book. Any
omissions will be rectified in subsequent printings if notice is given to the publishers.

Tel: 01865 888058 www.heinemann.co.uk

Contents

Which religious tradition?

In this paper it is important to be prepared to answer questions by referring to **two** religious traditions. The term 'religious traditions' refers to the six main world faiths - Buddhism, Christianity, Hinduism, Islam, Judaism and Sikhism or the major Christian traditions of Anglican, Orthodox, Protestant and Roman Catholic. This means that you may answer the paper by studying two different religions, for example, Christianity and Islam or Buddhism and Sikhism or Hinduism and Judaism. Please remember that within the religions you have chosen there may be more than one opinion on an issue. This is known as the diversity of opinion (viewpoints) within a religion. For example, within Christianity you may explain the teachings by saying something like 'Roman Catholics believe that it is always wrong because …. but Baptists believe that it depends on the circumstances because ….'.

The alternative approach is to choose Christianity on its own. If you choose this option you must be aware of two different Christian perspectives. An example of this would be to study the Roman Catholic and Anglican traditions. You would then include in your answer the Catholic and Anglican (Church of England) teachings and beliefs on a particular issue. The Protestant tradition includes different denominations such as Baptist, Methodist, Quakers and Salvation Army. Any denomination that is a member of the World Council of Churches is acceptable but answers on groups that are on the fringe of Christianity for example Mormons, Rastafarians, Jehovah Witnesses may not receive credit.

Your course

The course consists of two sections.

Section 1 is entitled 'Nature and expression' and is divided into three parts:

- Nature of truth and spirituality

- Claims to truth

- Some ways of expressing spirituality in society.

For the first part (Nature of truth and spirituality) you need only refer to one religious tradition. In the rest of the paper the examiners are expecting you to refer to two religious traditions.

Section 2 is entitled 'Religious responses to contemporary issues' and is divided into six parts:

- Religious attitudes to Matters of life

- Religious attitudes to Matters of death

- Religious attitudes to Drug abuse

- Religious attitudes to Media and technology

- Religious attitudes to Crime and punishment

- Religious attitudes to Rich and poor in society

The exam paper

The time allowed for this paper is 1 hour 45 minutes. During this time you are required to answer four questions. A question will be divided into several parts and you must answer every part. The first question (A1) is compulsory. This question will be on Section 1 of the syllabus - Truth and spirituality.

In Section B answer any three questions from B2 to B7. For example, you may wish to answer B2 on Matters of life, B4 on Drug abuse and B6 on Crime and punishment. Do not forget to read each question carefully before you start to answer it. You need to relate the information you know directly to the question being asked. Each question is marked out of 20 and the maximum mark for the paper is 83. You will be awarded up to 3 marks for quality of written communication (QWC). Good QWC marks will be awarded if you:

- ensure that your writing is legible (use a blue or black ink or ball-point pen) and spell, punctuate and use grammar correctly

- use religious technical terms where appropriate

- use a suitable structure and style of writing for example write in sentences and paragraphs.

Quotations

Learn two or three quotations from sacred texts or general religious principles and, if appropriate, one statement or teaching by a religious leader or authority. Some examples will be given in this book, but you should use the ones you have spent two years studying. Do not waste time trying to learn unfamiliar texts.

How this book is organized

Each section begins with 'What do I need to know?' which outlines information you will need to answer examination questions on the topic.

Margin features

Did you know?
Short pieces of information that are useful additions to your knowledge and can be used as examples in examination answers.

Hints and tips
Brief guidelines designed to assist revision and examination technique.

Exam watch
Brief tips to help you achieve better marks in your exam.

Beware
Tips to help you avoid commonly made mistakes in the exam.

Key ideas
Short points that summarize the main points in a section.

Action point
Brief exercises that you can practise to help you revise.

Read more

Suggestions for further reading to help you add more detail to your answers. These may also direct you to another section of the book where passages or topics are explained in more detail.

Key words

Important words and terms are in bold print the first time they appear in the book. Definitions can be found in the Glossary on pages 61–2. You should learn these and be prepared to explain them.

Questions

Each section ends with practice questions with the number of marks in brackets. This guides how much you should write.

Mark	Requirement
1	Write a simple one-word answer or a short sentence
2	'Give *two* reasons…' = write two simple points 'Explain…' = make one simple point with a sentence to explain it
3	Make one simple point, explain it and give an example
4 or more	Write continuously (see below)

Questions worth 4 marks or more are usually marked on levels of response. The examiner decides which level you reached in your answer and awards the marks attached to that level.

Questions worth 5 marks (evaluation questions) usually begin with a controversial statement and ask, 'Do you agree? Give reasons for your answer, showing that you have thought about more than one point of view.' Some also say, 'Refer to religious teachings in your answer.' These are always marked on levels of response. You cannot reach Levels 4 and 5 unless you refer to more than one point of view. You cannot reach Level 5 without referring to at least one religious argument.

The nature of truth and spirituality

What do I need to know?

- The different types of truth – scientific, historical, moral, spiritual – and the methods used to determine each type of truth.
- The meaning of 'spirituality' – awe, mystery, inspiration, creativity, **value**, meaning and religious **faith**.
- The truth claims of spirituality – **sources of authority**.
- How spirituality is expressed.

The different types of truth

Scientific truth

All scientific truth is based on a combination of:

- **evidence** – data on which to establish whether it is true or not
- the use of **reason** to develop a theory or **hypothesis**
- repeated testing/experiments to confirm the hypothesis.

Once the hypothesis or theory is confirmed, the result is a scientific truth or scientific law, for example, the law of gravity. All scientists have to be prepared to change, modify or reject a theory in the light of new evidence. For example, Charles Darwin produced a theory of evolution but there is not enough evidence to prove it to be a scientific truth. Scientists claim to have some proof and the probability (likelihood) is that the theory of evolution is correct but it is not a certainty (established beyond all doubt).

Historical truth

Historical truth is based on:

- evidence – information about past events gathered from contemporary documents, artefacts and so on (the facts)
- the use of reason and interpretation in order to understand the significance of past events.

There can never be one definitive explanation of past events because historians bring their own individuality and their own prejudices into their interpretation of the evidence. For example, some historians will regard suicide bombers as freedom fighters, while others will see them as terrorists. Also, historians look for new evidence to either support or refute their understanding of past events.

Moral truth

Moral truth is based on the teachings of **religious leaders** or **sacred writings** or on **abstract reasoning**.

Many people would say, 'Deliberately killing someone or deliberately stealing are *always* wrong.' These moral truths are called **moral absolutes**. Most people who believe in moral absolutes are members of a religious group.

action point

Think of experiments that you do in the science laboratory – do they fit the summary of scientific truth?

action point

Could you ever really know why President Kennedy was assassinated?

Others may say, 'Deliberately killing someone or deliberately stealing are *not always* wrong; it depends on the circumstances.' These people rely on their abstract reasoning to decide whether something is right or wrong.

Spiritual truth

Spiritual truth is based on personal belief or a faith that is rooted in personal reflection or meditation on one's experiences. These reflections or meditations may be linked to the teachings of sacred writings or, in particular **religious communities**, are linked to particular religious leaders or authorities.

The nature of spirituality

Spirituality is another way of talking about the **spiritual dimension** of life. It contrasts with what is called the **material dimension**.

People who live only for the 'now' and who find pleasure in acquiring possessions, are said to be 'materialistic'. People who believe in something greater and more meaningful than what we see, touch, hear, smell and taste, are said to be 'spiritual'.

Some people have a spiritual experience, which fills them with a sense of awe, wonder or mystery. This may have resulted from:

- watching a sunset or sunrise
- listening to a piece of music
- touching the skin of a new-born baby
- looking into a cloudless sky at night.

These experiences may inspire people to create a work of art or poetry or music.

The spiritual dimension of life also concerns value and **relationships**. Spirituality can give people an appreciation of the value of the world and of human life.

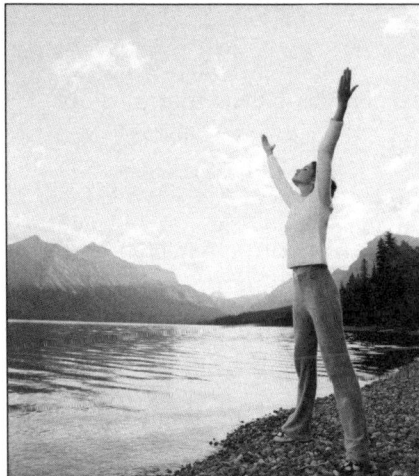

The truth claims of spirituality

Spiritual truth cannot be shown to be true in the same way that a scientific truth can be proved; that is, by making a theory or hypothesis and proving it by repeated testing or experiments. So why do so many people have religious faith or belong to a religion?

Believers say, 'My faith answers most, if not all, of the questions I have about life, death and how I should live.'

Many people who are sceptical want some kind of proof or evidence that the religion is true. Believers might say, 'Give it a try and see if it "works" like it does for me.' This approach is rather scientific because it demands repeated testing. Each day people act on beliefs that cannot be proven.

✔ **action point**

Are there any actions that are always wrong or right, or bad or good?

key ideas

People who believe in spiritual truths will say that the truths of science and history cannot, in themselves, give a sense of meaning and purpose for life. They are important for helping us to understand our world but, without an all-embracing spiritual truth, they leave us with no sense of eternal destiny.

✔ **action point**

How might a spiritual belief affect a person's attitude to the use of violence?

key ideas

Faith means being so convinced about something that you are willing to act on it even though you cannot prove it.

Claims to truth

The six major world religions offer answers to people's questions about life, death and how to live. Some religions encourage members to actively share their faith with others (for example, Christianity and Islam). In other religions, the members simply live out their faith and other people might be attracted to discover for themselves if the faith suits them (for example, Buddhism).

All religions have sources of authority that define and explain the particular religion. These are:

- sacred writings
- religious leaders
- **traditions**
- **conscience**.

Sacred writings

The most important sources of authority are the sacred writings or **holy books**. They contain the beliefs and teachings of the religion.

Some religions have one holy book:

- Islam – the **Qur'an**
- Sikhism – the **Adi Granth** (or Guru Granth Sahib)
- Judaism – the **Tenakh**
- Christianity – the **Bible**.

In Buddhism and Hinduism, believers may refer to one or more holy books, depending on the particular tradition they belong to.

- Buddhism – The Tipitaka or Pali Canon (containing the Vinaya Pitaka, Sutta Pitaka and Abhidhamma Pitaka)
- Hinduism – The Vedas, Puranas, Bhagavad-Gita, Ramayana, The Laws of Manu.

These holy books were written many centuries ago. Sacred writings have to be studied and interpreted.

Religious leaders

Religious leaders have been specially trained, chosen or elected to teach, advise and care for believers. They help believers apply the religion's teachings in their daily lives.

Christian leaders are given various titles, such as minister, pastor, priest and elder. In some Christian traditions or denominations, there are also leaders with more authority than the priest or minister. In the Roman Catholic tradition, there are bishops, archbishops, cardinals and the Pope. The Pope is the Bishop of Rome and head of the Roman Catholic Church. Christians believe that these religious leaders are chosen or called by God.

Hinduism encompasses a wide variety of belief traditions or sects with only a few basic, but important, shared beliefs, such as reincarnation. Each

beware

You must refer to *two* religious traditions when answering the remaining questions in this section or you will lose marks.

action point

- Make sure you know the names of the sacred writings for two religious traditions you have studied.
- What makes a holy book special? Can writings that are so old be of any use to us today?

action point

Make sure you know the religious leaders of *two* religious traditions you have studied.

tradition has its own religious leaders who are usually called **Guru** (teacher) or **Swami** (master).

Traditions

Certain 'events' or ways of doing things in a religion that date back to an earlier time are known as 'traditions'.

It is traditional for Christians to give up something during Lent to show the importance of Easter. Many Christians will fast for a day or more, or give up eating chocolate for forty days. This helps them to remember the suffering Jesus endured on the cross and the reasons for his death. Beautiful cathedrals and churches containing paintings, sculptures, icons and so on express the spirituality of Christians for example The Sistine Chapel in the Vatican in Rome contains a painting of the Last Judgement. Thousands of hymns and songs express their love of God. Countless books have been inspired by their beliefs for example Pilgrims Progress, the Narnia series and testimonies of those who have had spiritual experiences.

Buddhists meditate to empty the mind of all negative thoughts. Thoughts of anger, greed and ignorance can be replaced with thoughts of peace and tranquillity. There are three types of meditation - Metta, Samatha and Vipassana meditation. Buddhist monks create mandalas (patterns and images in coloured sand) to express their spirituality. Beautiful shrines are created in the temples or homes containing rupas (images of the Buddha).

Hindus celebrate a festival called **Holi**. They remember, especially, the god Krishna and the way he played tricks on people. Today, many Hindus throw coloured water or powder over each other in fun. Large beautiful temples have been built to celebrate Hinduism. Many have several shrine rooms and each shrine usually has a canopy over it. The shrines are beautifully painted and pandits (priests) look after them. They bathe the murti and dress the image in royal robes and flowers. Hindus also show their spirituality by their devotion and meditation.

Muslims have created some beautiful mosques, for example the Dome of the Rock in Jerusalem, as an expression of their faith. Mosques with their domes, minarets, calligraphy and geometric artwork dominate the skyline in many Muslim countries. Statues and paintings are not allowed but they are beautifully decorated and form an inspired setting for the Muslim congregation as they perform their rakahs (prayer movements) five times each day.

Examples of spirituality being shown by Jews include the discipline of accurately and beautifully hand writing the Torah scrolls. The Torah scrolls, with their beautifully designed mantle (cover), get paraded during the services.

Sikh musicians inspire the worshippers in the gurdwara. The ragis sing and play devotional music. The gurdwaras are beautifully decorated and the Guru Granth Sahib is covered by beautifully produced Romallas (fine clothes) when it is not being read.

> ✓ **action point**
> Make sure that you know a tradition for *two* religious traditions you have studied.

Conscience

One source of authority for many religious people is their conscience. Many people believe our conscience is made up of the things we learn as we grow up in a particular culture or social environment. It 'develops' without us realizing it. Following our conscience makes us feel 'at peace' and we feel a sense of 'guilt' if we do not follow it.

Others believe that conscience is something every human being is born with. It 'teaches' us what is right and wrong; for example, all human beings know 'deep down' that it is wrong to kill another human being.

For religious people, the conscience is a spiritual voice or the voice of God that is there to guide us when we might be confused about what to do in a certain situation.

Spirituality in society

There are three different ways people express their spirituality: expression of individual commitment, support of voluntary organizations and membership of a faith community.

Expression of individual commitment

Individuals show their spirituality through their use of symbolism. This may be seen in artefacts, ritual objects and physical movements. It involves showing **piety** (dutiful devotion to God and observance of religious principles). Believers express their spirituality by being pious, for example, carrying out acts of devotion such as kneeling, bowing and prostrating. It may involve focusing on particular objects, such as statues, paintings or writings, in prayer or meditation.

Piety requires discipline, as it is a regular practice and not something that is done occasionally. It may involve mysticism, which is a system of thoughtful prayer and spirituality that aims at gaining direct contact with God. The spinning action of the whirling dervishes, the Sufism group within Islam, is an example. Others use design, painting, sculpture, writings or some other creative way to express their personal belief.

> ✔ **action point**
> Can you list symbolic objects and actions and how they are used in the two religious traditions you have studied?

Support of voluntary organizations

Religious people express their spirituality by becoming involved in voluntary work on behalf of others. Examples include becoming a volunteer helper with Caring at Christmas or The Cyrenians (who provide accommodation for homeless people), becoming a first aider with the St John's Ambulance service, raising money for Christian Aid or Oxfam, becoming a supporter of Friends of the Earth, doing Voluntary Service Overseas (VSO), and so on.

Lay Buddhists support the work of the bhikkhus (monks) by making offerings of food. They regard gifts that are freely given and voluntary work as a source of great merit.

Christians organize many charities such as Christian Aid, Tear Fund, CAFOD and World Vision. The Salvation Army is well known for its work to help the homeless and those in need of care and attention. Jesus encouraged his followers to help those in need by his example and teaching. He healed the sick and taught that anyone in need should be helped, for example in the parable of the Good Samaritan (Luke 10: 25–37) and the parable of the Sheep and Goats (Matthew 25: 31–46).

Many Hindus donate up to ten per cent of their income to help the poor and/or become involved in charity work. Hindus believe that voluntary work results in the gaining of merit.

Muslims are encouraged to support those with genuine need and have many charities such as Islamic Relief and the Red Crescent. Muslims recall the charity of Muhammad by remembering those in need as they fast during Ramadan and give Zakah (two and a half per cent of their income) to the poor, this is one of the Five Pillars.

There are many Jewish organizations that help those in need including Jewish Care, United Jewish Communities, the Norwood Orphanages and Jewish hospices. Voluntary work is encouraged among all branches of Judaism.

Sikhs believe that karmic reward is received by those who are involved in voluntary work for the good of the community. Sikhs support helping the poor by providing a free kitchen (langar), shelter for the homeless, and carrying out other aspects of charity work.

Membership of a faith community

Many people express their commitment and spirituality by joining a religious community and sharing in that community's way of living.

Buddhists may become a bhikkhu or bhikkuni, attend the local temple, or go on retreat.

Christians may join a denominational church, go to live in a monastery, attend events such as Spring Harvest, or spend time at the Taize community in France.

Hindus have various forms of religious communities as well as the mandir or temple.

Muslims attend the mosques and take part in the pilgrimage known as the Hajj.

Jews become members of their religious community through attendance at the synagogue.

Sikhs follow the lifestyle of the religious community that attend the gurdwara and the langar.

The communities provide **pastoral support** and guidance for those who attend and there are opportunities for **corporate worship** (worshipping together, sharing in their beliefs). Part of the work of the communities involves helping others, and in most religions **witnessing** (telling others what God has done for them) and **evangelizing** (spreading the message to others).

✓ **action point**

Are you able to describe and explain how members of *two* religions you have studied show their commitment to that community?

hints and tips

Remember to refer to *two* religious traditions in your answers (unless the question states otherwise or it is obvious that it is not required; for example, it says 'Give *one* example …').

Short questions

a Give *one* example of what historical truth is based upon. (1 mark)

b What is meant by 'conscience'? (2 marks)

! beware

Take note of the marks given for each part of the question. Do not spend a long time giving a lengthy explanation if it is a one or two-mark question.

Examination type questions

a Give two examples of sources of authority for religious believers. (2 marks)

b 'Things that were written centuries ago in a religion should not influence what the believers do now.' Do you agree? Give reasons for your answer, showing that you have thought about more than one point of view. (5 marks)

Student's answer

a Sacred writings, for example, Guru Granth Sahib, and religious leaders, for example, a priest.

b The main sources of authority in Sikhism and Christianity are their sacred writings and so they are very important even though they were written a long time ago. After the ten human gurus, the Guru Granth Sahib became the living guru (as instructed by Guru Gobind Singh). The contents teach Sikhs to meditate on the name of God and its teachings encourage followers to lead purposeful lives as useful members of society. The teachings are of central importance to the life, work and worship of the Sikh community. The fact that it was written a long time ago is not regarded as important because it is seen as alive — the living guru.

In Christianity, the Bible is regarded as the Word of God revealed to humans over many centuries. As its source is God then it is seen as the truth and is regarded as timeless (for all people of all generations). It is seen as useful for guiding people to do what is right and for correcting errors. On the other hand, people may argue that the teachings do not include topics that are of great importance in the twenty-first century. Times have changed but the writings have not. What was appropriate behaviour 2000 years ago may not be relevant now when we have major problems resulting from smoking, abortion, drug abuse, and so on. So these writings are outdated.

I think that sacred writings should influence believers' behaviour now because it sets the right standards. The idea of loving your neighbour as you love yourself is just as relevant today as it was when it was written.

Examiner's comments

a Sacred writings and religious leaders identified. Mark: 2/2

b A very good answer, showing both sides of the argument and drawing a conclusion. Good examples/reasons included with reference to Sikh and Christian teaching. Mark: 5/5

Examination practice

Explain *two* ways in which religious believers show their spirituality. (4 marks)

Checklist for revision

	Understand and know	Need more revision	Do not understand
I know the different types of truth.	☐	☐	☐
I understand the methods used to determine each type of truth.	☐	☐	☐
I understand the meaning of 'spirituality'.	☐	☐	☐
I understand the truth claims of spirituality.	☐	☐	☐
I know and understand the different religious sources of authority.	☐	☐	☐
I know the meaning of 'conscience'.	☐	☐	☐
I understand how spirituality is expressed.	☐	☐	☐

1 Matters of life

What do I need to know?

- Beliefs about when life begins.
- Beliefs about who is responsible for life.
- Implications of development in medicine.
- Implications of medical research in the areas of human **genetic engineering**, embryology, cloning, transplant surgery and blood transfusions.
- Artificial methods of causing pregnancy, and surrogacy.
- The concept of the **sanctity of life**.

When does life begin?

Some people believe that this physical life is only a stage in our total existence. They believe that we existed before the birth of our present body and will exist after our body dies. Their beliefs suggest that there is part of us (for example, the soul or spirit) that may go through many lifetimes. This might have been in a lower life form or as a human being. This idea is reflected in the belief of reincarnation.

Some people argue that life starts at the moment when the sperm fertilizes the egg. At this moment, a new life, distinct from that of the parents, is given, with a unique genetic code. Other suggestions include:

- when the embryo becomes implanted into the wall of the womb
- when the primitive streak (first signs of the backbone) appears, which shows whether it is one or more individuals (after about fourteen days)
- when the mother first feels the baby move
- at the first heartbeat
- when the foetus is **viable** and could survive outside the womb
- when the baby is born.

Buddhists believe that being born in human form is rare and so is very precious. All living things are caught in **samara** (the cycle of birth, death, and rebirth). So life has already begun before conception in a previous existence.

Christians believe that God is the creator of life and that humans have a special relationship with him and that we are made in God's image - Genesis 1:26. Psalm 139:13–15 suggests that God not only creates us but knows us while we are developing in the womb. Roman Catholics believe that life begins at conception. Some Christians, for example Methodists, are not so sure that in the very earlier stages of pregnancy you can say that life has truly begun.

Hindus believe that Brahman is the source of all beings and that the atman (soul) is part of Brahman. As the soul never dies, life has already begun

Modern medical research and techniques have caused many people to be concerned about the morality of new developments. For example, is it morally right to use embryos for research?

action point

When do you think life begins? Your answer may influence your opinion when considering the use of embryos for medical research and genetic engineering.

action point

Who do you think is responsible for life? Religious believers (except Buddhists) believe that it is God. Do you think that if God creates life scientists have any right to interfere in the production of children or in the alteration of genes? If God does not exist, is it legitimate for any medical research or experimentation to take place?

before conception in a previous existence. All life is caught in the cycle of birth, death and rebirth (samsara) until **moksha** (spiritual liberation) is reached.

Muslims believe that Allah creates human life and provides the gift of children. 'He gives daughters to whom He will and sons to whom He pleases' Surah 42:49. Life begins at inception - the fusion of the sperm and the egg. Life and the spirit are not the same and some Muslims believe that the soul is breathed into the foetus on the 120th day of pregnancy.

Jews believe that each person is unique and valuable and life is a gift from God. He knows us before we are born (Psalm 139:13,15) and gives us a purpose for our lives (Jeremiah 1:5). Life does not truly begin until the baby is half way down the birth canal.

Sikhs believe that God is the creator of all life. There exists in each person the 'divine spark' (the soul). The soul is part of God and will be reabsorbed into Him after liberation takes place from the cycle of birth, death and rebirth (**mukti**). Life has already begun before conception is a previous existence (pre-existence).

Fertility treatment

Fertility treatments may be used to help couples who are infertile. Treatments include the following methods.

AIH

Artificial insemination using the husband's sperm. Doctors collect semen samples from the husband and these are artificially placed in the neck of the woman's womb.

AID

Artificial insemination of a donor's sperm. The same technique as AIH is used *but* the sperm donor is not the husband.

IVF

In vitro fertilization: the sperm and egg are put together to achieve fertilization in a test tube. Up to three of the resulting embryos are put into the woman's womb in the hope that a pregnancy will occur. Twenty-seven per cent of all IVF births produce two or more babies. One in 80 children born in Britain today are test-tube babies.

The Human Fertilization and Embryology Act 1990

This Act includes provisions to regulate research using human embryos. It covers:

* research using human embryos

* the storage of eggs, sperm and embryos

* fertility treatment that uses donated eggs or sperm (for example, AID) or embryos that are created outside the body (IVF).

Surrogacy

This is when a woman has a baby for another woman. She may become pregnant either by sperm donation from the father or another man.

The Surrogacy Arrangements Act 1985

- It is a criminal offence to advertise surrogacy in any way.

- It is illegal for payments to be made to a company or agency who assisted in the surrogacy arrangements.

The Human Fertilization and Embryology Act 1990 states that:

- the surrogate mother cannot be forced to give up her child

- the child must be genetically related to at least one of the commissioning parents

- the commissioning parents must both be over eighteen and married to each other

- no money other than expenses must be paid in respect of the surrogacy arrangements.

Six weeks after birth, the intended parents can apply for a parental order for full and permanent parental rights over the child.

In Buddhism, each individual may choose whether or not to use IVF or other forms of medical help to start a family. There are no grounds in Buddhism to say that it is either immoral or irreligious to have fertility treatment.

Roman Catholics do not support fertility treatments and surrogacy. They believe that if a couple does not conceive through sexual intercourse, then God has decided that they should not have children. Most Protestant denominations accept AIH and IVF, but AID is not considered desirable. AIH and IVF are acceptable because the parents are married and it is not important how the pregnancy began.

If the couple cannot conceive without help, medical aid is allowed. Hindus do not object to AIH. AID is unacceptable: this is because it poses problems for tracing the male ancestry and so children would not know what caste they belonged to.

IVF and AIH are allowed, but AID is forbidden because using sperm from an unknown donor is seen as similar to committing adultery. Surrogacy is opposed because 'No one can be their mother except those who gave them birth' (Qur'an, surah 58: 2). Having children is seen as very important in Islam, but Muslim men are allowed by the Qur'an to have up to four wives and so surrogacy is not seen as necessary.

For childless couples, non-Orthodox Jews accept AIH. Most Orthodox Jews oppose masturbation, so AIH is seen as unacceptable by some rabbis. AID is definitely not acceptable, as the donor may be the unknowing father of several children. It could lead to marriage between unsuspecting close relations and is regarded as a form of adultery. IVF treatment is acceptable if a couple are unable to have children through normal sexual intercourse. The idea of surrogacy is not acceptable to Jews as the idea of motherhood is very important in Judaism.

Sikhs desire a son to carry on the family name and to care for the parents in their old age. If the married couple fail to conceive by natural means (sexual intercourse), fertility treatments such as IVF and AIH are permitted. Sikhs believe that procreation should be between husband and wife, so AID and surrogacy are not allowed.

Transplant surgery

This is the name given to the procedure of replacing an organ in one person's body with the equivalent organ from someone else. Often the replacement organ is from someone who has died. Transplant operations save or improve the life of thousands of people each year as organs like hearts, kidneys, livers or corneas are replaced. The organ has to be accepted by the recipient's system, which can be a major problem and anti-rejection drugs have to be used. Recent medical advances have led to 'xenotransplantation' – this is the use of organs from genetically modified animals, for example, hearts and lungs from pigs.

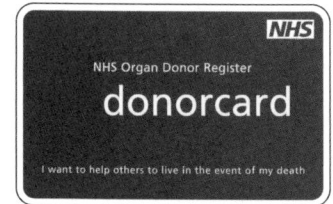

Blood transfusions

If a person loses blood, for example, through an accident or operation, doctors may give them blood provided by blood donors. Blood comes in four main types – O, A, B and AB – and it is essential to give a person the correct type or their body will reject it and they could possibly die.

Buddhists believe that organ donation, transplant surgery and blood transfusions are matters of individual conscience.

Most Christians including the Greek Orthodox Church support organ donation, transplants and blood transfusions. The principle of 'Love your neighbour as you love yourself' (Mark 12: 33) is applied. Jehovah's Witnesses allow transplant surgery but not blood transfusions.

The donating of organs for use in transplant surgery is left up to the individual. Hinduism does not forbid the use of body organs or blood if it helps to relieve the suffering of others.

Muslims allow transplant surgery but the organs must be donated by humans. Organs from animals may be used. Muslims allow blood transfusions but it is only permissible for genuine need.

Jews strongly support and encourage organ donation for use in transplant surgery. Jews are also encouraged to be blood donors.

Blood transfusions and organ transplants are acceptable within the Sikh religion. The donation of a cornea, kidney, lung or other organ from relatives would be regarded as an act of kindness.

Human genetic engineering

Scientists will soon be able to produce 'designer babies', selecting the genes for sex, height, eye, hair and skin colour, intelligence and athleticism, for example. The procedure for modifying the genetic make-up of cells is known as genetic engineering. Genes are made from DNA (deoxyribonucleic acid). The collective name for all these genes is the **human genome**. The genome is like a recipe book or blueprint for each individual person. Scientists have recently mapped the human genome and are developing the ability to treat gene disorders. Faulty genes cause disease as they give out incorrect instructions in cells. **Gene therapy** involves replacing a defective gene with a new one.

Cloning

Cloning is the production of genetically identical (sharing the same nuclear gene set) individuals. There are two very different procedures.

1   Embryo cloning involves the removal of one or more cells from an embryo and encouraging the cell to develop into a separate embryo. It has the same DNA as the original. This type of cloning has been carried out with animals, for example, Dolly the sheep.

2   Therapeutic cloning involves taking the DNA out of an embryo and replacing it with DNA from another individual. The process kills the embryo but the stem cells may be grown into a replacement heart, liver or skin, and so on. This process is still being developed. If successful, the organ's DNA would match the patient's DNA, so overcoming rejection problems.

> **did you know?**
>
> Dr Ian Wilmut claimed that his first 276 attempts to clone a sheep resulted in malformed animals. Dolly the sheep was his 277th attempt.

Cloning humans

This is not legal but some scientists are eager to clone humans.

Arguments in favour of cloning humans include the following.

- It will allow selective breeding to improve the human race.

- Parents could choose the sex of their offspring.

- Cloning creates life from life and is just an extension of IVF (*in vitro* fertilization).

- It is no more 'playing God' than other fertility treatments.

- Changing a single two-cell form of life into two one-cell forms of life and discarding any unwanted cells is not murder. At this very early stage, true life has not begun.

Arguments against cloning humans include the following.

- Cloning is 'playing God' and interfering with nature.

- Cloning denies the sanctity of life.

- A clone would not be a 'real human' with its own separate identity.

- The clone may not have a soul. If a soul enters the body at conception and the fertilized ovum is a human being, then a cloned embryo may not have one.

- Life starts at conception, so killing embryos is murdering unborn children.

- Attempts to clone a human may result in malformed babies (as with the first attempts to clone a sheep).

- The government has banned human cloning as being morally and ethically unacceptable.

Buddhists are concerned that genetic engineering brings risks and could do irreversible damage to life. No scientific experiment can assess whether there is a risk that genetic engineering or cloning might affect the path to enlightenment. The karma from the harming of life in developing gene therapy or cloning may cause problems in the future.

Roman Catholics believe that embryo research threatens the sanctity of life. Anglicans and most Protestants support research, under license, on embryos up to fourteen days old, providing the embryos are not created just for scientific research. Most Christians do not oppose the cloning of animals but do not support the idea of cloning humans. Roman Catholics regard it as a threat to the uniqueness that God has given us. Christians totally oppose any idea of creating a human clone for 'spare parts'.

Hindus believe that human genetic engineering should only happen under strict conditions, as changes may be difficult to reverse. If done with good intentions, cloning may bring benefit, but if it is done for selfish reasons, for example, greed or power, it may bring severe karmic consequences. Human cloning brings real dangers and unanswered questions; for example, will the soul be held up from being reborn while part of the body remains alive?

Embryos should not be created for research but those leftover from IVF treatment may be used. Most Muslims give a definite 'no' to human cloning as it may undermine family ties and social order and raises questions about the identity and individuality of the person.

Spare embryos from IVF treatment or aborted foetuses present no problem as a source of stem cells for use in developing treatments. Cloning plants or animals or to produce replacement organs may be acceptable, but most Jews regard the possibility of cloning humans as 'playing God'.

The production of embryos for scientific research is not allowed, but spare embryos from, for example, IVF treatment, may be used. Most Sikhs are unsure about whether cloning will bring benefit to the human race, either physically or spirituality.

exam watch

Remember, you are expected to show that you are aware of the beliefs and teachings of *two* religious traditions.

beware

Do not give a one-sided answer in the evaluation questions; always give a balanced view from both sides of the argument.

Short questions	
a What is meant by 'transplant surgery'?	(2 marks)
b What do the abbreviations 'AIH' and 'IVF' mean?	(2 marks)

Examination type questions

a Which Act includes provisions to regulate research using human embryos? (2 marks)

b 'Cloning is wrong and should be banned.' Do you agree? Give reasons for your answer, showing that you have thought about more than one point of view. Refer to religious teachings in your answer. (5 marks)

Student's answer

a The Human Fertilization and Embryology Act 1990.

b Some people argue that cloning is 'playing God' as the process involves killing an embryo. It interferes with nature and the sanctity of life. Experiments have resulted in many deformed animals and it is not acceptable to make deformed human babies. We do not know the full implications of cloning. For example, Dolly the sheep seems to have aged prematurely and is dead, and would a human clone have a soul?

On the other hand, cloning could have benefits such as producing organs for transplant that will not be rejected by the patient. Also, coupled with genetic engineering, it could result in improvements to the human race or animal kingdom. This is a complex issue and I have worries about the cloning of humans. In the wrong hands, this could be very dangerous.

Examiner's comments

a A correct answer. Mark: 2/2

b Arguments for and against are given and the complexity of the issue is recognized. However, it lacks reference to the beliefs and teachings of religious traditions. It is nearly worth 4 marks but some arguments could be developed further, for example, why 'this could be very dangerous'. Mark: 3/5

Examination practice

Explain why some religious people are *either* in favour *or* against genetic engineering. (5 marks)

Checklist for revision

	Understand and know	Need more revision	Do not understand
I am aware of beliefs about when life begins and pre-existence.	☐	☐	☐
I know about the different types of fertility treatments.	☐	☐	☐
I understand the meaning of surrogacy.	☐	☐	☐
I know and understand the meaning of:			
• human genetic engineering	☐	☐	☐
• embryology	☐	☐	☐
• cloning	☐	☐	☐
• transplant surgery	☐	☐	☐
• blood transfusions.	☐	☐	☐
I understand the beliefs and teaching of *two* religious traditions towards the above issues.	☐	☐	☐

2 Matters of death

What do I need to know?

- The role of the family and community in caring for the terminally ill and elderly.
- The work of homes for the elderly and hospices.
- The use of life-support machines and artificial means of supporting life.
- A definition of death.
- What is meant by sanctity and quality of life.
- The issue of self-determination in relation to euthanasia and suicide.
- The difference between active and passive euthanasia.
- The debate about whether euthanasia should be made legal.

did you know?

One hundred years ago, five per cent of Britain's population was aged over 65. Now it is almost twenty per cent and rising.

Problems facing the elderly

- Failing health – diseases such as arthritis, rheumatism, cancer, strokes, and so on, become more of a problem. This causes a heavier demand on the National Health Service (NHS).
- Financial difficulties – the old age pension is equivalent to about fifteen per cent of the average male earnings and around 70 per cent of pensioners rely on it as their only income.
- Loneliness – over 2 million pensioners live by themselves.

Caring for the elderly

In previous generations, the **extended family** took care of the elderly. Several generations lived together or were close enough to help each other. Today, most live in **nuclear families** (the parents plus the children). The elderly grandparents may live miles away and caring for them can be a problem.

Help from the community

The community provides help in the following ways:

- community care schemes including home helps, the meals-on-wheels service and support from the social services
- local authorities have warden-controlled units (sheltered accommodation) where the residents have their own independence. An alarm button alerts the warden if help is required
- Social Services Departments run residential homes for those with more serious disabilities
- private residential and nursing homes provide twenty-four hour nursing care.

Hospices

Patients suffering from a terminal illness might be cared for in a hospice. In this type of hospital, the aim is to relieve suffering and control their symptoms in the most effective way. This approach is known as **palliative care**. The emphasis is to try to give the patient a good quality of life for their final days. Patients are encouraged to talk about and prepare for death. Most hospices in Britain are Christian foundations.

Buddhists believe in respecting the elderly and celebrating their wisdom. They encourage elderly people to stay in their homes with their families for as long as possible, but where this is impossible, Buddhists work with agencies, such as hospices, which care for the terminally ill.

Christians believe the elderly should be treated with respect and honour: 'Respect your father and your mother.' (Exodus 20: 12) The experience and wisdom associated with age is recognized. Senior citizens need love and care whether they are living in a nuclear family situation or in an elderly people's home. Many churches provide visitors, senior citizen groups, homes or sheltered accommodation for members of their denominations.

Hinduism teaches that old age is to be respected: 'Let your mother be a god to you. Let your father be a god to you.' (Taittiriya Upanishad 1.11.2) The elderly should be cared for by the extended family.

Muslims consider it an honour, blessing and opportunity for great spiritual growth to look after and care for parents. In Islam, serving one's parents is a duty second to prayer and it is the right of the elderly to expect it. To send them to a home for the elderly is thought to be unkind and disrespectful.

Judaism teaches that it is important to 'show respect for old people and honour them' (Leviticus 19: 32). Families are encouraged to look after aging parents but Jewish communities have homes that provide care for the very elderly and the very frail. In Britain, Jewish Care provides residential, day, home, dementia, nursing and respite care.

Respect for elders is a key principle of Sikh society. It is regarded as the duty of sons to care for their parents. The home and the help of those who meet in the local gurdwara are seen as the primary support for the elderly.

Definition of death

Death is usually defined as occurring when the heart stops beating and the lungs stop working. This is known as cardio-respiratory death.

The sanctity of life

This means that life is special, even sacred, because it is God given and so should be valued and protected.

The quality of life

Many people believe that a good quality of life is more important than the length of a person's life. Someone enjoying a good quality of life will be able to enjoy life to the full. Poor quality results from suffering, illness, extreme poverty, loneliness, and so on.

---

did you know?

There are over 2000 Macmillan nurses and 300 Macmillan doctors working in hospices in Britain. They not only provide palliative care for patients but help the families come to terms with the impending death of their loved ones.

action point

Use the Internet to find out more about Dame Cecily Saunders and Macmillan nurses.

action point

Do you think someone who is 'brain dead' is still really alive? Brain death means the irreversible loss of all brain function. A person who is 'brain dead' cannot breathe without the help of a life-support machine. Should patients in a permanent vegetative state (PVS) be allowed to die?

Religious beliefs about life after death

Buddhists believe in rebirth (again becoming), so this life is not the end. What happens in the next life depends on the karma that they have obtained. The return is to one of five or six realms of existence - gods, human, animal, hungry ghosts or hell. For those who have obtained enlightenment they may escape to nirvana.

Christians believe that the soul will be judged on the Day of Judgement and believers will join God in heaven because Jesus won the victory over death by his resurrection. Heaven is described as a wonderful place. Non-believers will be separate from God in hell. Roman Catholics believe in purgatory (a place between heaven and hell) where souls go to be cleansed (purified) of their sins.

The aim of the Hindu is for their atman (soul) to obtain freedom from samsara (the cycle of birth, death and rebirth), obtain moksha or liberation and be near or reunited with the Supreme Reality of Brahman. If moksha is not reached the body which atman occupies in the new life is determined by karma from a previous existence.

Muslims look forward to the resurrection of the body. The soul enters into eternal life and is taken by Aza'il, the angel of death, to wait in barzakh until the Day of Judgement (Akhirah) or Resurrection. On this day Allah judges each person and paradise awaits as a wondrous reward for believers. Unbelievers are consigned to Jahannam (hell), a place of torment.

There is little mention of afterlife in the scriptures and there are different beliefs within Judaism. The Talmud warns against speculation about it as 'no eye has seen it'. Most Jews look forward to the Messianic Age when the Kingdom of God will be established on earth. On Judgement day God will reward the righteous and the unrighteous will be sent to hell (gehinnom). Here they will be cleansed from sins so that they can enter the presence of God.

Sikhs believe that the soul is part of the Eternal Soul (God) and it has existed since creation. Eventually it will be reabsorbed into God but in the meantime it goes through a series of births, deaths and rebirths as it evolves from lower forms. Heaven and hell are not seen as place of judgement but are experienced on earth.

Suicide

This is the term used to describe the act of killing oneself. There are nearly 150,000 attempted suicides in Britain each year. Over 6000 result in death – about three-quarters of these are men.

Euthanasia

The word 'euthanasia' comes from the Greek words '*eu*' and '*thanatos*'. Together these words mean 'a gentle (good) death'. Sometimes it is called **mercy killing**. Euthanasia is illegal in Britain but is allowed in some countries, for example, Holland.

There are various forms of euthanasia.
- Passive euthanasia: this means the taking away or withholding of treatment with the intention of ending life; for example, not giving life-prolonging drugs. In

key ideas
Some people argue that there are times when the quality of life is so poor that it is justifiable to end that life to prevent further suffering.

some instances, patients are given pain-relieving treatment in such high doses that they may die more quickly. This is known as the 'double effect'.

- Active euthanasia: this is when a doctor deliberately intervenes to end life, for example, by administering a drug.

- Voluntary euthanasia: this means helping someone to die at their request because they are suffering terribly, for example, from an incurable disease.

- Involuntary (compulsory) euthanasia: this is when someone else makes the decision; for example, when a doctor or the state kills a person without their permission.

Pressure groups such as the Voluntary Euthanasia Society take the view that people should have the right to make their own decision about their own death. They suggest that members make a 'living will' to declare that they do not wish their lives to be artificially prolonged in the event of a terminal illness or if they are in a permanent state of unconsciousness. Some carry a medical emergency card, which states that if there is no reasonable prospect of recovery, then they do not wish to be resuscitated or to have their life prolonged artificially.

Die with dignity!

Murder!

Humanely end suffering!

The right to live!

The right to die!

Life is a gift from God!

My life, my choice!

Don't play God!

The arguments for euthanasia

- Death with dignity is better than a long, lingering, painful death.
- Death may be a 'happy release' for relations.
- Animals are put down rather than allowing them to suffer, so why not humans?
- With an ageing population, can we afford to take care of old and infirm people?
- Doctors are aware when there is no hope of recovery.
- An injection can quickly and humanely end suffering.
- If the quality of life is very poor, why should a person not choose to die?

The arguments against euthanasia

- Euthanasia is a form of murder.
- Every person has the right to live.
- It is 'playing God' to decide that a person's life should end.
- Life is a gift from God and is sacred.
- Euthanasia devalues life by making it disposable.
- The doctors may make an incorrect diagnosis.
- The Hippocratic Oath forbids doctors from killing their patients.
- Modern drugs ensure that no one suffers to an unbearable degree.
- If we allow voluntary euthanasia, it is the slippery slope to compulsory euthanasia.

Taking life is against the first precept – to keep from harming any living thing. Care and support for the dying is encouraged, but decisions about euthanasia may not be easy. Suicide or euthanasia for the wrong reason will lead to negative karma and bring about more suffering for all those involved in a future life. If the motive for euthanasia is for Right Intention, then it becomes a possibility. Some Buddhists argue that each case needs to be considered on its own merit.

Acts 17: 26 state that God has fixed our life span and He alone has the right to take it away and so suicide is regarded as wrong. Christians recognize that the euthanasia debate is a complex one and there are a variety of Christian views. Roman Catholics believe that euthanasia is always wrong: 'Without the consent of the person, euthanasia is murder. His consent would make it suicide. Morally this is a crime, which cannot become legal by any means.' (Pope Paul VI) Others believe that passive euthanasia (for example, the withdrawal of drugs) may sometimes be justified as death may bring release from suffering and eternal life in heaven.

Helping a person to take his or her own life is both a crime and a sin: 'The one who tries to escape from the trials of life by committing suicide will suffer even more in the next life.' (Yajur Veda 40–3) Hindus believe in doing their duty (**dharma**) by providing care for the terminally ill. To help someone else to die would attract bad karma and suffering in future rebirths. To prevent this from happening, the motive for euthanasia would have to be totally selfless.

'Allah fixes the time span for all things.' (Qur'an, surah 53) To decide when a person should die is to try to 'play God'. Terminating life and suicide is forbidden. If a person suffers, it is the will of Allah who is testing them and not a reason for euthanasia. Muslims believe that after death the worthy will join Allah in Paradise, a place of great delight and reward. The Hadith says that those who kill themselves by the sword, poison or throwing themselves off a mountain will receive punishment on the Day of Resurrection.

Life is a blessing given by God (Genesis 1: 27). God the creator decides when we are to be born and when we should die. However desirable it may seem, active euthanasia is playing God: 'He sets the time for birth and the time for death.' (Ecclesiastes 3: 2) Passive euthanasia is seen by some in a different

Consider the following:

- Should a person have the right to self-determination (that is, being able to decide for himself or herself what happens to them)?
- Does he or she need protection from making a decision, which once acted upon cannot be reversed?
- Should doctors have the right to end such suffering by giving the patient a lethal injection?

light, as it prevents the postponing of death by artificial means. Suicide is regarded as a serious sin. Those who commit it are buried in a separate part of the cemetery.

Most Sikhs oppose euthanasia and suicide, as it is God who gives and takes life and His will should not be interfered with: 'God sends us and we take birth. God calls us back and we die.' (Guru Granth Sahib 1239) If a person is in a permanent vegetative state, then to stop giving life-preserving drugs might be acceptable.

hints and tips

When asked for a definition, develop your answer by giving an example.

Short questions

a What is a hospice? (2 marks)

b What is meant by 'palliative care'? (2 marks)

Examination type questions

a What is meant by the term 'euthanasia'? (2 marks)

b 'Children should look after their ageing parents, not the government.' Do you agree? Give reasons for your answer, showing that you have thought about more than one point of view. Refer to religious arguments in your answer. (5 marks)

Student's answer

a Euthanasia means 'mercy killing' or gentle death. It is legal in some countries when people are suffering from an incurable illness. It is not the same as suicide.

b Muslims regard it as the duty of the children to look after their ageing parents. To send them to a home is seen as disrespectful. This seems to me to be an old-fashioned attitude. In today's world, children may not have the time or money to look after their parents. The children need a life of their own.

I understand that it is right to honour your parents as Jews believe, but you can take it too far. When parents become very elderly, they may be too frail for their children to manage, but I do not think children should just expect the local authority to look after them if they are reasonably healthy.

I think children have a responsibility to their parents but might well need help from the community and local government. It should be a partnership.

Examiner's comments

a The student clearly understands the term and is able to put it within a context. Mark: 2/2

b Reference is made to both Islam and Judaism. Several good points are included but could have been developed further by adding some reference to sacred texts, for example 'Honour your father and your mother' (Exodus 20: 12), 'Show respect for old people and honour them' (Leviticus 19: 32), 'Be kind to parents' (Surah 17: 23). Arguments made for and against are included and a personal opinion given. Mark: 4/5

Examination practice

Explain the difference between passive and active euthanasia. (5 marks)

Checklist for revision

	Understand and know	Need more revision	Do not understand
I understand the role of the family and community in caring for the terminally ill and elderly.	☐	☐	☐
I know about the work of homes for the elderly and hospices.	☐	☐	☐
I know about the use of life-support machines.	☐	☐	☐
I understand what is meant by sanctity and quality of life.	☐	☐	☐
I understand the issue of self-determination in relation to euthanasia and suicide.	☐	☐	☐
I understand the difference between active and passive euthanasia.	☐	☐	☐
I understand the main arguments concerning whether euthanasia should be made legal or not.	☐	☐	☐

3 Drug abuse

What do I need to know?

- Religious beliefs and teachings concerning the mind and body.
- The use of caffeine, alcohol and tobacco.
- The use and effects of illegal drugs.
- Drugs taken for social and recreational purposes.
- Drugs taken to enhance performance in sport.
- The classification of drugs.
- The debate about the legal status of drugs.

What is a drug?

A drug is a substance that, when taken into the body, alters the way the body works and may change the way we feel. Some drugs are:

- depressants – slows down the central nervous system
- stimulants – speeds up the central nervous system
- hallucinogens – affects our senses and alters the way we perceive or see things.

Social drugs

An individual might take drugs as part of their social life with others. These are known as social drugs; for example, drinking alcohol at the pub with friends or having a cup of coffee with guests. Some drugs taken for social reasons are not legal; for example, the taking of Ecstasy at a rave.

Recreational drugs

Drugs used by people for non-medical reasons as part of leisure or relaxation time are known as recreational drugs. It includes legal drugs such as caffeine, alcohol and tobacco, and illegal drugs such as amphetamines, cannabis, Ecstasy, heroin, ketamine, LSD, and magic mushrooms.

Performance enhancing drugs

Some people are prepared to take drugs to improve their performance in sport. Despite the dangers to health and the risk of being banned from their sport, some competitors wish to gain an advantage over their rivals. Attempts are made to catch the drug cheats by regular testing of competitor's urine or blood. Some high-profile sportsmen and women have tested positive for banned substances and been punished by the relevant sporting bodies. For example, Canadian Ben Johnson was stripped of his 100 metres sprint world title on testing positive for a banned drug.

did you know?

Not all substances can be detected, for example, human growth hormone, and as a result some drug cheats get away with breaking the law in their sport. Some may be taken 'innocently'; for example, some athletes and footballers who have been tested positive for nandrolone have vigorously protested that they have not knowingly taken the banned substance.

Drugs used to enhance performance include:

- erythropietin (increases stamina)
- oxyglobin (helps the body obtain and use more oxygen)
- steroids (helps build muscle bulk)
- stimulants (reduces tiredness and fatigue).

Legal drugs

Caffeine

Caffeine occurs naturally in coffee and tea and is added to most soft drinks. It is an addictive drug.

- It stimulates the central nervous system and makes a person feel more energetic.
- It makes the body produce more urine.
- Large doses increase the risk of heart attacks.
- It can cause restlessness, sleeplessness, nervousness, excitement, a flushed face, palpitations, diarrhoea and rambling flow of thought and speech.

Tobacco

There are about 1.1 billion smokers in the world – around seventeen per cent of the total population. About 6000 billion cigarettes are smoked each year. The government receives nearly £8 billion a year from tax on cigarettes – about two per cent of its total tax revenue. ASH (Action on Smoking and Health) aims to educate people about the dangers of smoking. Eight out of ten smokers begin under the age of twenty and the majority wish they had never started.

- There are over 4000 harmful chemicals in tobacco cigarettes including aluminium, ammonia, arsenic, carbon monoxide, copper, lead, mercury, nicotine and zinc.
- Smoking causes 80 per cent of lung cancer deaths and seventeen per cent of deaths from heart disease.
- Smoking-related illnesses cost the NHS over £400 million a year.
- 17,000 children under five are admitted to hospital each year because of the effects of passive smoking.
- 120,000 people die each year in the United Kingdom because of smoking.

Alcohol

About 90 per cent of adults in Britain drink alcohol. People who are addicted to alcohol are called alcoholics. People who do not drink alcohol are called teetotallers. The government receives about £7 billion a year from tax on alcohol – about 1.8 per cent of its total tax revenue.

- Drinking too much causes severe damage to the liver and the brain.
- Between 8–14 million days are lost by industry each year because workers are unfit to work due to excessive drinking.

> ✔ **action point**
>
> Make a list of reasons why sporting authorities wish to catch those who take performance enhancing drugs. Make sure you know some of the types of drugs used and their effects.

- It costs the NHS around £150 million to deal with alcohol-related health problems.

- One in four males admitted to hospital are there because of alcohol abuse.

- Around 28,000 people die each year in the United Kingdom because of alcohol abuse.

- Around 60,000 people are found guilty of, or cautioned for, drunkenness each year.

Alcoholics Anonymous is a group of people who have overcome their addiction and now help others to recover from alcoholism.

Smoking is not a right or perfect action because of the damage that it does to the smoker. Also, a non-smoker who inhales the smoke has their health put at risk. The fifth precept is to abstain from taking drugs and alcohol that cloud the mind. Most Buddhists do not drink alcohol because of this.

Christians do not encourage smoking, as it is unpleasant for non-smokers and a health hazard. Some Christians are teetotallers (non-drinkers), for example, members of the Salvation Army. They believe that 'the right thing to do is to keep from … drinking wine, or doing anything else that will make your brother or sister fall' (Romans 14: 21). Many Christians believe in moderate drinking and avoid getting drunk. Jesus did not oppose drinking; for example, he turned water into wine at a wedding feast and he told his followers to share wine as they remember him. Paul encouraged Timothy to take some wine for medical reasons: 'Take a little wine to help your digestion.' (1 Timothy 5: 23)

Many Hindus are smokers, but Hindu teaching does not encourage the use of substances that have a harmful effect on health and smoking is banned at Hindu temples. Hindu teaching does not agree with alcohol abuse as it causes people to lose control and do evil things. Alcohol addiction is seen as preventing spiritual progress: *'All those which produce molasses and such intoxicants are to be forbidden by those who desire spiritual rewards.' (Manusmriti)*

During Ramadan, Muslims are not allowed to smoke. Smokers are encouraged to give up because it is addictive and is a danger to health. In the Qur'an (surah 2: 195), Allah says, '… do not with your own hands contribute to your destruction.' Muslims believe that the harm alcohol causes is far greater than any good that comes out of it: 'Believers, wine and games of chance, idols and divining arrows, are abominations devised by Satan. Avoid them.' (Qur'an, surah 5: 90) Muhammad said that intoxicants are the mother of all vices and it is forbidden by the Qur'an and the Hadith to take anything that would cause you to lose control of yourself and your mind.

Many Jews do smoke, although the numbers are declining. Many rabbis discourage smoking because of the dangers of lung cancer and other illnesses. Drinking alcohol is part of the Jewish tradition. Wine is drunk to celebrate the Sabbath and festivals like Pesach and Purim. But 'drinking too much makes you loud and foolish. It's stupid to get drunk' (Proverbs 20: 1).

Smoking is listed in the Rahit Maryada (Code of Conduct) as one of the four sins (kurahits). The Rahit Maryada also states that Sikhs should not use intoxicants, for example, alcohol: 'By drinking wine one loses sanity and becomes mad, loses the power of discrimination and incurs the displeasure of God.' (Adi Granth: 554) The Gurus also forbade the drinking of alcohol.

Illegal drugs

The illegal drugs trade is an international multi-billion pound industry. Criminal gangs make a fortune from smuggling drugs into Britain each year. Drugs can be:

- injected – either into the muscle, under the skin, or into a vein (mainlining)

- smoked – the smoke is inhaled into the lungs where it is absorbed into the bloodstream

- inhaled – sniffed up the nose (for example, glue sniffing) or inhaled through the mouth

- swallowed or chewed – taken as a pill, a tab, or chewed.

Drugs and the law

The Misuse of Drugs Act 1971, the Drug Trafficking Offences Act 1986, and the Intoxicating Substances (Supply) Act 1985 are the three laws that deal with drug abuse. Illegal drugs are classed according to how dangerous they are. Class A drugs are the most dangerous, then Class B, and the less dangerous are Class C drugs.

- Class A drugs include crack cocaine, Ecstasy and heroin. The maximum penalty for possession is seven years imprisonment and/or a fine. The maximum penalty for supplying Class A drugs is life imprisonment and/or a fine.

- Class B drugs include amphetamines. The maximum penalty for possession is five years imprisonment and/or a fine. The maximum penalty for supplying Class B drugs is fourteen years imprisonment and/or a fine.

- Class C drugs include anabolic steroids. The maximum penalty for possession is two years imprisonment and/or a fine. The maximum penalty for supplying Class C drugs is five years imprisonment and/or a fine.

Drug	Effects	Risks
Cocaine (Coke) Class A	Mental: exhilaration; hallucination then fatigue; depression Physical: increased blood pressure, heart rate and body temperature	Addiction; death from heart attacks, strokes; respiratory failure; panic attacks
Heroin (smack) Class A	Mental: users get a 'rush' or 'buzz' Physical: vomiting and headaches; loss of appetite; constipation	Addiction; overdosing; comas; choking on vomit; mental health problems
Ecstasy Class A	Mental: mild euphoric 'rush' Physical: increased brain activity; anxiety; panic and confusion	Overheating; dehydration, which can be fatal; liver, kidney and brain damage
Cannabis/ marijuana Class C	Mental: euphoria; hilarity Physical: increased heart rate; loss of short-term memory; confusion; apathy; sleepiness	May induce a coma; bronchitis; cancer; psychological dependence; increased risk of infertility

Solvents

This term describes a variety of everyday items such as aerosols, correction fluid, glues, nail varnish remover, paint and petrol.

did you know?

Research suggests that more people are now taking illegal drugs than ever before. Young people in Britain are reported to be taking up to five times more illegal drugs than the average for the rest of Europe.

They contain chemicals that when sprayed, or sniffed, alter the state of mind of the user. Using solvents this way is illegal and dangerous.

Why do people take non-medical illegal drugs?

Why do people experiment with dangerous drugs? The reasons include:

- Peer or family pressure. Friends experimenting with drugs pressurise group members to join them. If older brothers or sisters take drugs the younger members of the family often copy them.

- Pressure from dealers. Drugs are expensive and dealers need customers to finance their business or their habit.

- It is part of the dance and youth culture. Research suggests that many who go clubbing or to 'raves' take drugs like Ecstasy.

- For excitement. If something is dangerous or illegal some people want to try it because they know they should not.

- To assert their independence. Some people may be going through a stage of rebellion against authority and their parents and want to show that they are grown up.

- For an escape. Drugs help some people escape from the real world and forget their problems.

- To feel good. Some people take drugs for the pleasure that they feel. When the feeling goes they take more drugs to try and recapture it.

- To seek a mystical experience. Some people hope to have a 'religious' experience while under the influence of the drugs.

- They are addicted. Once started they cannot stop. This may be physical or psychological addiction.

Arguments for legalizing all drugs

- Legalizing drugs will stop the drug cartels making massive profits.
- Drugs will be less appealing because they will not be 'forbidden fruit'.
- Drug enforcement costs millions of pounds.
- Society is losing the war on drugs so they might as well be legal.
- Some illegal drugs are possibly no more harmful than alcohol or tobacco.
- Drug users would have easier access to clean needles and so it would reduce the risk of HIV and Hepatitus C.

Arguments against the legalizing of drugs

- Legalizing drugs would send the wrong message to society.
- Many would start with soft drugs and then move on to hard drugs.
- The government has a duty to protect society.
- More people would become addicts and the cost to the NHS would increase.
- Deaths from drug abuse would increase.

action point
Go to www.heinemann.co.uk/hotlinks to visit some websites which will help you to find out more about the different types of illegal drugs and their damaging effects. Why do so many young people try illegal drugs when they know how dangerous they are?

action point
List reasons for and against legalizing cannabis (see student's answer at the end of this section for help).

Buddhists emphasize the need to be alert in body, speech and mind in order to think about the consequences of their actions and be able to meditate properly. Addicts break the fifth precept and use illegal drugs to get away from the truth. This is not acceptable.

Christians believe that they should glorify God in their bodies and drug abuse does not do that: 'Surely you know that you are God's temple and that God's Spirit lives in you!' (1 Corinthians 3: 16) Christians believe that drug addicts should be helped to overcome their habit. Groups such as the Salvation Army do not judge drug addicts or alcoholics but try to help them break free from the condition they are in.

Some Hindus, including many sadhus (holy men), have taken drugs for meditative purposes, but many Hindus are opposed to any addictive drugs. Hindu sacred writings forbid the use of illegal drugs and anything that will affect the mind or cause dangers to health: 'Bewildered by numerous thoughts, entangled in the web of delusion and addicted to the ratification of desires (like consuming intoxicants) the stupid people fall into a foul hell.' (Bhagavad Gita)

Muslims believe that Allah owns their bodies and anything that 'covers' or affects the mind is not allowed (haram). Illegal drugs are strictly forbidden and severe punishments are enforced in Islamic countries. Performance enhancing drugs is seen as cheating and dishonourable.

Drug abuse and performance enhancing drugs are forbidden, as Jews are not allowed to destroy their own body, endanger their own lives, or inflict damage upon other people.

All substances, which are physically or mentally harmful, are banned: 'Intoxicated with opium, cannabis and alcohol, people forget good deeds and … wander in the life of confusion.' (Bhai Gurdas Ji 3916) The Nihangs of Punjab, who are the defenders of the historic Sikh shrines, are an exception. They take cannabis to help in meditation.

Argument for legalizing cannabis

- It appears to have medicinal properties which may help MS sufferers.
- It would allow the police to focus on tackling the problem of more dangerous drug abuse.
- It has already been legalized in countries like the Netherlands.
- Tobacco and alcohol are legal and are arguably as dangerous.

Arguments against legalizing cannabis

- It is a gateway drug (users may move on) to more dangerous drugs like heroin.
- Smoking cannabis causes cancer and lung disease. It has higher tar content than tobacco.
- Research suggests that it affects the brain and users are six times more likely to develop schizophrenia than non-users.
- Users risk serious psychological dependence.
- Users are more likely to have accidents or get into situations they do not feel able to control.

beware

It is easy to leave out religious teachings. Religious teachings gain you marks – make sure you include them from *two* religious traditions.

Short questions

a What is a drug? (2 marks)

b Name two Class A drugs. (2 marks)

Examination type questions

a Name two (non-medical) drugs, which are legal. (2 marks)

b 'Cannabis ought to be legalized.' Do you agree? Give reasons for your answer, showing that you have thought about more than one point of view. Refer to religious arguments in your answer. (5 marks)

Student's answer

a Caffeine and tobacco.

b Many people think that searching people for cannabis wastes police time. They could be concentrating on 'hard drugs' like heroin or arresting the drug pushers. Many people believe that cannabis is not addictive and is no more dangerous to health than cigarettes. Also, it helps multiple sclerosis sufferers. To make it legal would take the excitement out of smoking it and it has already been reclassified as a Class C drug.

Others say that it is a gateway drug. It is the start of a slippery slope that leads on to more dangerous Class A drugs such as heroin. Users are risking their health as it causes loss of short-term memory and illnesses similar to those suffered by smokers, for example, bronchitis and lung cancer. It can also cause poor performance at school or work.

I think it should not be legalized except perhaps to use as a medicine, as Christians believe that the body is the temple of the Holy Spirit and should not be abused. I agree with the Christian idea that our bodies are a sacred gift from God and so should not be harmed.

Examiner's comments

a Both answers are correct. Mark: 2/2

b Good arguments for and against and a final concluding paragraph bringing in the student's personal opinion and religious teachings. Mark: 5/5

Examination practice

Choose *two* religious traditions. For each, explain their attitude towards:

a alcohol

b illegal drugs. (10 marks)

Checklist for revision

	Understand and know	Need more revision	Do not understand
I know and understand religious beliefs concerning the mind and body.	☐	☐	☐
I know how caffeine, alcohol and tobacco are used and the dangers associated with them.	☐	☐	☐
I understand the use and effects of illegal drugs.	☐	☐	☐
I understand what is meant by social and recreational drugs.	☐	☐	☐
I understand the problem of drug cheats in sport.	☐	☐	☐
I understand how and why drugs are classified.	☐	☐	☐
I understand the debate about whether or not illegal drugs should be legalized.	☐	☐	☐

4 Media and technology

What do I need to know?

- The different types and accessibility of the media.
- The debate about the effects of the media on children.
- How the media is controlled including advertising standards, categorization of films, censorship and the TV watershed.
- The beliefs of two religious traditions concerning media and technology.
- The nature, purpose and range of religious broadcasting on terrestrial and satellite TV.

key ideas

The media has a major influence on how we view and live our lives. Many religious people are concerned that the media can undermine moral standards, for example, causing violence and immorality.

The media

The term 'media' (or mass media) refers to the way information is communicated to the general public. This may be in written form, for example, newspapers, magazines and books, or in transmitted or oral form, for example, television, cinema, radio, the Internet and music. The media is able to inform, educate and entertain.

The Press

- Around 14 million newspapers are sold in Britain each day.
- Newspapers are described as either 'tabloid' (for example, *The Sun* and *The Mirror*) or 'broadsheet' (for example, *The Times*, *The Telegraph* or *The Guardian*) because of their size and shape.

The development of information technology has allowed an explosion in the number of books and magazines that are now being published.

The influence of the media on society is enormous. People's opinions and attitudes may be swayed by media campaigns. Newspapers can repeat the same sort of message and influence their readers. The private lives of famous people are exposed to press coverage, for example David Beckham. Many people are worried that the paparazzi (freelance photographers who pursue celebrities to photograph them to sell to newspapers and magazines) go too far.

Television and radio

- On average, people watch over three hours of TV every day.
- Young people watch on average over 25 hours of TV each week.
- 99 per cent of homes have a TV set.
- By 2010, most TV's will be digital.

Terrestrial TV (programmes available through the normal aerial) includes BBC1, BBC2, ITV, Channel 4 and Channel 5, and there are many more channels available via digital TV stations, for example, BBC News 24.

The development of cable and satellite TV has meant a huge increase in the availability of programmes. Viewers pay subscription fees and companies such as Sky provide a large range of programmes, from sport to films. A network of national and local radio stations are also available. Some are part of the BBC and others are financed by advertisers, for example, ITV.

The watershed

BBC and ITV programmes before 9pm are supposed to be suitable for a general audience including children. After the 9 o'clock watershed, there may be scenes of sex, violence and strong language but a warning is given. Broadcasters recognize that terms of racial abuse, sexual swear words, abusive names relating to disabilities and the misuse of names considered holy by believers, for example, 'Jesus Christ', can cause great offence. Many religious people are concerned that some television programmes go beyond what is decent and promote what they regard as negative rather than positive values.

Buddhists are concerned about the intention or purpose behind the media, for example, in TV programmes. They ask the following type of questions: does it encourage harm to living things, criminal activity, the use of offensive language, abusive sexual relationships, or the taking of drugs? Does the material try to overcome the Three Evils or does it encourage greed, hatred and ignorance?

Some Christians are concerned that the media have challenged and weakened traditional Christian values providing, for example, inappropriate role models for young people. Respect for marriage and the family, God and the Church has been undermined and the result is an increase in society of violence, bad language, drug abuse, criminal activity, pornography and immorality. In some programmes, church leaders (vicars, ministers) are portrayed as pathetic figures who are out of touch with the reality of the world.

Hindus are concerned with the content of programmes that do not uphold moral values. In the Laws of Manu, it is stated: 'Non-violence, truthfulness, abstention from unlawfully taking what belongs to others, purity, and control of one's organs, Manu has declared these to be the sum total of the dharma of the four castes.'

Muslims look to the media to uphold the beliefs, teachings and moral values of the Shari'ah (Muslim Law). They are particularly concerned about the effects the media can have on the attitudes of young people who grow up in the United Kingdom away from the control of a Muslim society. Smoking, drinking alcohol, drug-taking, violence, immodesty, sexual promiscuity, adultery and homosexuality are all contrary to Muslim values.

The Jewish faith focuses on respect for God and His laws, the value of life and the importance of the family. The violence, sexual misconduct and abuse and devaluing of family life, which forms a part of some television programmes and films, goes against all the teachings of Judaism. As a historically persecuted minority group, Jews are very sensitive to stereotyping, the presentation of political issues in Israel, and how they are portrayed, even through comedy.

Sikhs look to the media to encourage young people to value marriage and family life and to steer them away from smoking, excessive use of alcohol, drug-taking, violence, immodesty, sexual promiscuity and adultery. Often the opposite is the case and Sikhs are concerned that television, magazines, and so on, can have a bad influence on people.

Blasphemy

In Britain there is a law on blasphemy, which protects the Christian religion. Blasphemy means to show contempt or disrespect for God. An example would be to use Jesus Christ as a swear word which is offensive to the Christian community. The act of abusing God's name breaks one of the Ten Commandments – 'Do not use my name for evil purposes, for I, the Lord your God, will punish anyone who misuses my name' (Exodus 20:7). This law is rarely used but a certificate was refused for the film *Visions of Ecstasy* because it showed St. Theresa of Avila having sexual feelings for the crucified Christ.

Blasphemy laws in Britain do not protect other religions although some people feel strongly that the law should be changed to either include all religions or be scrapped altogether. Sometimes films are made, or books written, that are deeply offensive to some believers. For example, many Muslims were upset when Salman Rushdie wrote a book called *Satanic Verses* in 1989. Muslims regard anything that speaks in a derogatory manner about Allah or Muhammad as blasphemous.

Music

Developments in technology have had an enormous effect on the music market. Vinyl gave way to cassettes and cassettes gave way to CDs. Recordings have been made of worship and religious songs by many of the different religious traditions.

Cinema

The British Board of Film Classification (BBFC) is responsible for film, video and DVD classification in the United Kingdom. Classification takes place according to their suitability for viewing by people of different ages.

Films are classified as follows:

U – Universal: suitable for all audiences four years and over.

PG – Parental Guidance: general viewing, but some scenes may be unsuitable for some children.

12 – no one younger than twelve unless accompanied by an adult.

15 – suitable for those fifteen years and over.

18 – suitable only for adults.

R18 – to be supplied only in licensed sex shops to adults of not less than eighteen years.

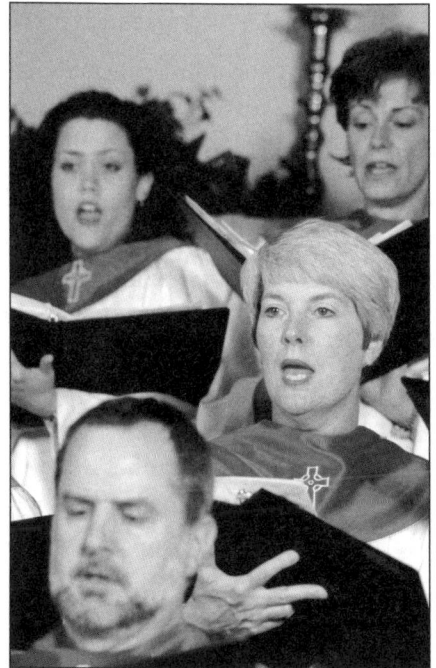

The Internet

This recent development in communication provides worldwide access to more than 400 million sites. The World Wide Web is normally accessed by computer via a telephone line. Over half the homes in Britain have access to the Internet and students are being encouraged to use the Internet at school and at home. It is like having access to an enormous library of information on every subject imaginable. It is ideal for obtaining information for projects and homework. Emails are now a very important method of communicating information for both individuals and companies. It enables cheap communication to be made almost instantly to virtually all parts of the world.

Although this communication revolution has a positive side, there are three major concerns about the Internet that religious people and others share.

1 Pornography: there is no control over what can be posted on the Internet. Access can easily be gained to pornography. Downloading some pornographic material is illegal in the United Kingdom if it is subject to the Protection of Children Act (1978), which prohibits indecent photographs of children.

2 Inaccurate or unsuitable material: As yet there is no universal system of checking, correcting and editing the information that is put on the Internet. Some of the information may be misleading, unhelpful or even destruction. Information about how to make bombs, obtain guns or perform criminal acts could be used by terrorists and criminals to devastating effect. Sensitive and confidential information occasionally appears and although the Internet is monitored for such sites and many eventually removed, the damage can already have been done.

3 Chat rooms: people 'talk' to total strangers who may not be telling the truth about themselves. There are great dangers in what can be suggested in these rooms, especially if it leads to meeting up with the person. A lot of personal information can be given away without knowing how the other person might use the information; for example, paedophiles can use the chat rooms to suggest meeting up with unsuspecting young people.

Buddhists realize that the Internet is a powerful tool for enabling people to find out about their faith. There are many sites on the Internet where people can learn about Buddhism. People can be instructed in meditation online.

Christians have been quick to see the potential of the Internet as a tool for informing people about their beliefs. Sermons can be obtained online and there are many educational sites and information about Christian organizations, for example, Christian Aid and the Salvation Army.

Hindus have created many websites devoted to their religion so that other Hindus may access information about their religion wherever they are in the world. Some sites are education based so that enquirers can find out more about Hindu teachings and sacred writings.

key ideas
Faith communities are able to use the Internet to inform people about their religion.

key ideas
There is concern about what is on the Internet, breaches of privacy by newspapers, and the content of many TV programmes.

The Internet is used as way of promoting Islam. A large number of sites exist, which contain the Qur'an and other teachings of Islam. Many also present the news from a Muslim perspective and give coverage to items from around the Muslim world.

Jewish organizations have been quick to make use of the Internet to transmit news and views. For a religion whose members are in communities around the world, this is a powerful way of keeping in touch with what is going on.

Sikhs use the Internet to promote religious observance and moral behaviour. Their sacred writings and also the Rahit Maryada (Code of Conduct) may be studied online. Sikhs make use of the Internet to inform members of the public of the beliefs of their religion.

Censorship

Censorship means subjecting the media to examination in order to control what is published or broadcast. As all the religious traditions have strong views about what is morally acceptable, they support censorship of the media. Many would like to see the censorship strengthened to prevent unsuitable material from being broadcast.

Controlling the Press

The Press adopts a system of self-regulation. This means it sets standards that its members must observe and it also deals with complaints. The British National Union of Journalists (NUJ) adopted a Code of Conduct in 1994. The Press Complaints Commission is an independent body that deals with complaints from the public about newspapers and magazines.

The Broadcasting Standards Commission

The Broadcasting Standards Commission deals with complaints from individuals. For example, people may claim that a television or radio programme has treated them unfairly or invaded their private life. The Commission considers complaints about taste, decency, violence and sexual conduct in programmes and advertisements.

The Obscene Publications Act 1959 and 1964 states that any piece of writing is obscene if its effect might be 'to deprave and corrupt' the people who are likely to read, see or hear what it contains.

The Telecommunications Act 1984 makes it an offence to send 'a message or other matter that is grossly offensive or of an indecent, obscene or menacing character'. Similar controls exist for sending material through the post.

The Advertising Standards Authority (ASA) has to make sure that advertisements are legal, decent, honest and truthful.

did you know? Mary Whitehouse set up the National Viewers' and Listeners Association (now known as mediawatch-uk) in 1964 over concerns about the effects of the media on people's morals and behaviour.

did you know? In 2000, the BBC broadcast 600 hours of religious programmes on the radio and 110 hours on television.

Religion and the media and technology

Religious publications, films and TV programmes are widely used to spread the message of their faiths. Satellite transmission means that radio and TV programmes can be broadcast around the world. A search of the Internet will produce thousands of websites about religion, spirituality and ethical and moral issues.

Religious broadcasting is controlled by The Broadcasting Act 1990. This requires the BBC, the Independent Television Commission (ITC) and the Radio Authority to act responsibly in terms of religious broadcasting and to have respect for listeners and their beliefs.

Programmes are required to reflect the worship, thought and actions of the mainstream religious traditions in the United Kingdom. This means that most British programmes will be Christian, but some may be aimed at the other main religious groups represented in this country.

Buddhists would appreciate more TV programmes that help people live according to the Eightfold Path, the Four Noble Truths and the Five Precepts. Much of what appears in the media encourages people to want a materialistic lifestyle rather than promoting simplicity, generosity and kindness.

Millions of people watch programmes such as *Songs of Praise* each week. Many elderly Christians who are unable to attend church particularly value worship programmes; but there is some concern about how religious leaders are often portrayed as figures of fun in TV dramas. In the United States, televangelism is very popular. Religious groups and sects own many channels there. Most use their programmes for bible study, preaching, televising services and hearing testimonies from believers.

The Mahabharata and Ramayana, with their battles between good and evil and their love stories, have made excellent film material. The BBC has an Asian Network on radio and both the BBC and other commercial channels have special programmes for the Asian community, which include aspects of Hinduism. Satellite channels such as Zee Television and Asianet broadcast in Hindi, English and Indian regional languages.

Muslims appreciate that good can come from the media in support of education and in broadening people's knowledge. Terrestrial TV often features special Islamic events, for example, the Hajj. Radio has made it possible for local Muslim stations to provide programmes in English and other languages to serve their communities. Radio Ummah also broadcasts worldwide via the Internet.

Most Jews would appreciate more time being devoted to religious programmes. They feel that their faith is often inadequately represented on terrestrial TV. Jews would value more programmes about Jewish life and culture as well as their religion.

Satellite TV is now used as a means of keeping members of the Sikh community around the world in touch with each other and it enables their own perspectives on issues to be presented. They often focus on particular concerns of Sikhs, such as the Punjab. There are also several Sikh radio stations, some of which broadcast on the Internet.

key ideas

Although the number of hours of television programmes has increased over the last decade, the number of hours devoted to religious topics has decreased. The faith communities are not happy about this.

hints and tips

Make sure you include religious arguments and views from *two* religious traditions in your evaluation answers. Give arguments for and against the statement and include reasons for your own opinion.

Short questions

a What does the term 'media' mean? (2 marks)

b What is terrestrial TV? (2 marks)

Examination type questions

a Explain what is meant by blasphemy. (2 marks)

b 'The Internet is dangerous because there is no censorship.' Do you agree? Give reasons for your answer, showing that you have thought about more than one point of view. Refer to religious arguments in your answer. (5 marks)

Student's answer

a Blasphemy means to show contempt or disrespect for God, for example, to use 'Jesus Christ' as a swear word.

b Practically anyone can put what he or she likes on the Internet. Terrorists can include instructions for making bombs; the porn industry has loads of sites, and few people check the accuracy of what is said. Religious believers say that it is dangerous because children can gain easy access and can have their minds polluted. Christians and Buddhists are concerned about the effect the Internet has in promoting materialistic values.

Others argue that the police do check sites and prosecute those who put child pornography on the Internet. Also, people do not have to access unsuitable sites and parents can erect 'firewalls' to prevent children from getting into dubious areas.

Examiner's comments

a A correct answer with example. Mark: 2/2

b Arguments for and against are given. The religious arguments need developing by explaining why Christians and Buddhists are concerned about 'minds being polluted' and the promotion of materialistic values'. Also, it requires a concluding paragraph that expresses the student's own views and reasons. Mark: 3/5

Examination practice

'There should be more religious programmes on TV.' Do you agree? Give reasons for your answer, showing that you have thought about more than one point of view. Refer to religious arguments in your answer. (5 marks)

Checklist for revision

	Understand and know	Need more revision	Do not understand
I know what is meant by the media and what it includes.	☐	☐	☐
I understand the concern about the effects of the media on children.	☐	☐	☐
I understand the issues concerning control of the media including:			
• advertising standards	☐	☐	☐
• categorization of films	☐	☐	☐
• the Internet	☐	☐	☐
• censorship	☐	☐	☐
• the watershed.	☐	☐	☐
I understand the beliefs of *two* religious traditions concerning the media and technology.	☐	☐	☐
I understand the nature, purpose and range of religious broadcasting on terrestrial and satellite TV.	☐	☐	☐

5 Crime and punishment

What do I need to know?

- Religious beliefs about punishment, repentance and forgiveness.

- Crime against the individual, property, the state and religion.

- Causes of crime.

- The aims of punishment.

- The issues concerning different forms of punishment.

- Effects of imprisonment.

- Treatment of young offenders.

- Parole and early release.

- Life imprisonment and capital punishment.

- Community service orders.

- Prison reform.

key ideas

A sin is the breaking of a religious or moral law. Religious offences vary from religion to religion but include such things as blasphemy (insulting God or sacred things) and the making of images of God.

What is crime?

A crime is the breaking of the law of the country. There are crimes against a person, for example, mugging and slander; crimes involving property, such as theft or fraud, and crimes against the country, such as selling state secrets or failure to declare earnings and pay taxes.

There are two kinds of offence:

- non-indictable: these are less serious offences; for example, motoring offences and petty theft

- indictable: these are more serious crimes; for example, rape and murder.

In Britain the law fits into two categories - criminal law and civil law.

Criminal law is when a person breaks the law of the country. The state takes action against an offender through the police and courts system. The Magistrates Courts deals with the less serious offences and the Crown Court is used for trying more serious criminal cases.

Civil law involves a dispute between individuals or groups. The courts may award damages (a sum of money) to one party, make a restraining order (ban someone from having access to see or visit someone) or settle disputes regarding wills, legacies, divorce and so on.

did you know?

- Since the early twentieth century, recorded crime has increased on average by over five per cent per year.

- There are over 5 million reported cases of crime each year.

- Around 100,000 persistent offenders are responsible for 50 per cent of Britain's crime.

Causes of crime

Why do people break the law?

- Social reasons: to join in with their friends and be one of the 'gang'.

- Environmental reasons: poverty, unemployment, lack of education and a deprived home background.

- Psychological reasons: human nature is naturally selfish and people always want more and to be more powerful than others. Some people commit crimes because of mental or emotional problems, boredom or hatred.

- Drug addiction: addicts may finance their drug habit through shoplifting or prostitution.

Aims of punishment

There are five main aims of punishment.

1 Protection
The public needs to be protected from law-breakers. Punishments such as imprisonment remove criminals from society so they are unable to commit further crimes.

2 Retribution
'Getting revenge' or 'getting someone back' is another aim. Criminals suffer for what they have done wrong so the victims feel that justice has been done.

3 Deterrence
The thought of a severe punishment may stop or deter the person from committing a crime.

4 Reformation
The aim is to change a criminal's ways and persuade them to become responsible citizens. Law-breakers may attend group therapy or be required to help the victims of their crime or carry out community service orders.

5 Vindication
Members of society need to respect the law. Without law there would be total chaos. Punishment is given to make it clear that the law is there to be taken seriously.

> **✓ action point**
> Make certain you understand each of the aims of punishment and consider which are the most important for *two* religious traditions you have studied.

Buddhists believe the roots of all evil are greed (lobha), hatred (dosa) and ignorance (avijja). The need to protect society and vindication is recognized but Buddhists do not believe in retribution as it goes against the Buddhist teaching of loving kindness (**metta**) and compassion (**karuna**). The ideal is to get the criminal to see their error and to reform (change their behaviour).

Christianity teaches that it is right to obey the government and uphold the laws of the country (Romans 13). Most Christians believe that punishment and forgiveness can go together, but there should be a strong emphasis on reform. The aim is to bring reconciliation between the criminal and society. This is not seen as being 'soft' on crime but trying to design the punishment so that it helps to rehabilitate the offender and change his or her behaviour.

Hindus are expected to avoid antisocial behaviour (**paapa**) as bad karma results from a wrong action. The purpose of the law is to protect people and to enable them to carry out their dharma (duty). In Hindu scriptures, the severity of the punishment depended on the caste of the criminal – the lower the caste, the more severe was the punishment. Laws are no longer based on caste but suitable punishment (danda) has three main aims – retribution, protection and reformation.

Muslims follow the Shari'ah (Islamic Law). They do not see punishment as a way to atone for sin, as only Allah can forgive. People need to be deterred from committing crimes and society must be protected from wrongdoing. Punishments may be severe: 'As to the thief, male or female, cut off their hands: a punishment by way of an example.' (Qur'an, surah 5: 41) Adultery may be punished by beating or stoning for example, a Nigerian Muslim woman, Amina Lawal, was condemned to be buried up to her neck and stoned to death on June 3 2003 because she had a child outside of marriage.

Jews believe in the rule of law and order and justice for all. Prevention and reform are at the centre of the Jewish approach to criminals. The aim is not retribution and vengeance, even though Exodus 21: 24 teaches 'an eye for an eye'. In the Talmud, it is referred to as paying money to make up for the wrong that has been done. Jews believe that if they repent of their wrongdoing and try to make amends for what they have done wrong (atonement), then God will be merciful and forgive.

Sikhs believe that the law needs to protect the weaker members of society from criminals. The key principle to good law is justice. Sikh teaching does not encourage retribution and retaliation but stresses the importance of trying to be like God who is without hatred (**nirvair**). Sikhs are encouraged to forgive and to work towards reforming a person so that they can become a useful member of society.

Young offenders

Once a young person has reached the age of ten, he or she is regarded as old enough to understand right from wrong and can be charged with breaking the law.

Types of punishment

- Community service orders: offenders do unpaid work for the community, for example, clean up graffiti or waste ground. Orders vary between 40–240 hours.

- Custodial sentences: offenders are sent to prison or detention centres.

- Fines: money is paid to the courts.

- Suspended sentences: these sentences (for example, a prison sentence) only take effect if the convicted person re-offends within a set time.

- Probation orders: offenders have to see a probation officer on a regular basis. This is to 'advise, assist and befriend' the offender and help them stay out of trouble. Failure to comply means the offender will find themselves back in court.

Britain no longer uses corporal (physical punishments, for example, caning) or capital punishment (the death penalty).

action point

Which aim of punishment do you think is the most effective? Why?

did you know?

Young people commit 40 per cent of the crimes in Britain and in 1998 there were 5283 boys aged under eighteen in custody.

did you know?

Britain's prisons are overcrowded, many are very old and others have problems with violent behaviour. Over 70,000 criminals are currently in jail; over 4000 are serving life sentences. The average term served by 'lifers' is approximately fifteen years. A concern is that a convicted murderer might murder again if released.

Parole

Many prisoners do not serve the full sentence given to them by the courts. A parole board considers the risk to the public of an 'early release' of the prisoner. The behaviour and co-operation of the person whilst in prison is considered.

Prison reform

Many people are concerned that in Britain we have a large prison population that is growing. In 2002 there were over 70,000 inmates and many of the prisons are extremely overcrowded. Britain has more prisoners per head of population than any other country in Europe.

Many argue that:

- too many people are sent to prison
- prison does little to reform a person, statistics show that most prisoners reoffend within two years of their release from prison
- mixing with other criminals reinforces criminal tendencies
- the whole family suffers and many marriages fail to survive
- ex-prisoners find it difficult to re-adjust to society and get employment when released
- each prisoner costs the taxpayer over £30,000 a year. This is much more expensive than other punishment options such as tagging or community service.

Others say that:

- if a person has lost their freedom, they cannot continue a life of crime
- other forms of punishment cannot offer such protection to the public
- it is important not to go 'soft' on criminals
- prisoners are given education and taught new skills which will help them on release
- taking away freedom teachers some people a lesson.

Organizations, such as the Howard League for Penal Reform and the Prison Reform Trust, campaign for improvements in prison conditions. They are worried that prisons are overcrowded and provide a hostile environment – on average, one prisoner commits suicide every five days.

Amnesty International

This is an organization that would like to see an end to capital punishment throughout the world. It also campaigns for the release of political prisoners and compiles list of those who are facing the death penalty. During 2001 over 3000 executions were reported as having taken place in 31 countries. The largest number of these took place in China.

Letters, petitions and emails are sent to governments requesting that death sentences are rescinded. For example, several million signatures were amassed

key ideas

Many believe that prison sentences are often not the best solution because on release more than half are reconvicted within two years.

action point

Find out more about the Prison Reform Trust, which was founded in 1981, by going to www.heinemann.co.uk/hotlinks and clicking on this unit.

during 2003 via email to ask the Nigerian government not to allow Amina Lawal to be buried up to her neck and stoned to death because she had committed adultery.

Alternatives to prison

Electronic tagging

This is widely used in the United States as an alternative to prison. Electronic ankle tags are attached to criminals so their movements can be checked. It may be linked to the home detention curfew scheme, where prisoners have to stay at home at night.

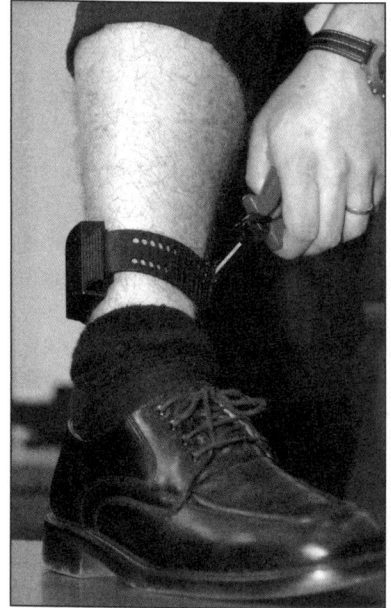

Advantages include:
- the low cost (about £4 a day)
- its flexibility; for example, shoplifters can be kept at home during shop opening hours
- the avoidance of separating families and offenders can still work.

Disadvantages include:
- technical problems – the equipment occasionally fails to work
- it is not suitable for dangerous criminals
- offenders might still continue their life of crime.

Community service

Are community service orders a 'soft' option or a way of benefiting the local community and saving money? Clearing areas of derelict land, the restoring of property, the cleaning of rivers, and so on, are some examples of projects carried out by offenders. It costs less than £2000 a year for a person to be given a community service order.

Capital punishment (the death penalty)
- Over 100 countries, including Britain, have abolished the death penalty.
- Where it exists, execution is usually by hanging, firing squad or lethal injection.
- The United States has about 3000 prisoners on death row.

Arguments against the death penalty
- Innocent people are sometimes executed.
- There is no evidence that the death penalty is more of a deterrent than life imprisonment.
- Locking someone away for life protects society just as well.
- Life is sacred. Who has the right to execute another person?
- Only God can really judge a human being.
- The death penalty is a barbaric punishment.

Arguments for the death penalty

- The death penalty may act as a deterrent to murderers.

- Terrorists and murderers deserve to die.

- The death penalty protects the public, as it stops the offender from being able to commit another serious crime.

- A 'life' sentence does not mean life (usually only about fifteen years).

- It is much cheaper to execute someone than to keep them in prison.

Some Buddhists support the use of capital punishment as a deterrent (providing it is rarely used) but most oppose it as it goes against the precept of not taking life. Buddhists are expected to show loving kindness. Imprisonment is supported for dangerous criminals but the emphasis is on providing opportunities for the person to learn from their mistakes and make amends. Offenders generate karma that punishes them in the future so the emphasis should be on reform.

Prisons are necessary to protect society but many Christians, for example, Quakers, are deeply concerned that prison can badly damage people. Many Christians believe that, with the exception of dangerous criminals, other forms of sentencing are preferable. Many support ideas to reform the prison system. Christians have different views on capital punishment. Some support it because it may act as a deterrent but most oppose it because innocent people might be executed by mistake.

Hindu teaching does not oppose capital punishment, for example, 'great criminals should all be put to death' (Vishnusmriti 5: 1). In the past punishments were severe, but many today believe that the death penalty goes against the principle of ahimsa (non-violence).

Most Muslims believe that two crimes should attract the death sentence – murder or if someone openly attacks Islam in such a manner as to threaten it. Muhammad accepted the justice of 'a life for a life'. The relatives of the dead person may instead choose to accept financial compensation and the offender may then receive life imprisonment instead of the death penalty: 'You shall not kill any man … except for a just cause. If a man is slain unjustly, his heir shall be entitled to satisfaction.' (Qur'an, surah 17: 33)

Jews recognize the need for prisons to protect society from criminals and rabbis visit and counsel prisoners and help prisoner's families. The Torah lists several offences that may be punished by capital punishment but it is very rarely carried out and exists primarily as a deterrent. Judaism sees it as important that the offender has the opportunity to atone for the wrong he or she has done.

Sikhs recognize that people need protection from dangerous criminals and so they accept the need to send some criminals to prison. Most Sikhs oppose capital punishment believing that executing a prisoner would be 'killing in cold blood'. Some believe that the threat of capital punishment may provide a deterrent to protect the rest of society.

hints and tips

If there is a difference of opinion within a religious tradition, make sure you mention it.

Short questions

a   What is a community service order?   (2 marks)

b   What is meant by 'parole'?   (2 marks)

Examination type questions

a   What is the difference between a sin and a crime?   (2 marks)

b   'Capital punishment ought to be brought back.' Do you agree? Give reasons for your answer, showing that you have thought about more than one point of view. Refer to religious arguments in your answer.   (5 marks)

Student's answer

a   A sin is the breaking of a religious or moral law such as taking God's name in vain. A crime is the breaking of a state law such as burglary.

b   Capital punishment was banned in this country because people thought it was barbaric and innocent people might be executed by mistake. Once a person has been executed, it is too late if future evidence shows that they were innocent or that the evidence was unreliable. For example, the Birmingham Six were released when investigations declared that the evidence of their trial was unreliable. If capital punishment had existed, the six might well have already been executed. It is also 'playing God', as only God has the right to end life.

On the other hand, some people would like to see it brought back to act as a deterrent to stop people committing murder. The Law of Moses says, 'an eye for an eye … a life for a life'.

I do not think bringing back the death penalty would make any difference as most murders are not premeditated and there is no real evidence to suggest that it is really a deterrent.

Examiner's comments

a   The candidate clearly understands the difference between a sin and a crime.   Mark: 2/2

b   Arguments are given for and against and the ideas are developed. There are some references to religious teachings but they need to be explained more fully for top marks. For example, an explanation of what the Law of Moses actually means when it says an 'eye for an eye …' in relation to the Jewish or Christian view on capital punishment.   Mark: 4/5

Examination practice

Explain the main aims of punishment.   (5 marks)

Checklist for revision

	Understand and know	Need more revision	Do not understand
I know about religious beliefs concerning punishment, repentance and forgiveness.	☐	☐	☐
I know about crime against the individual, property, the state and religion.	☐	☐	☐
I understand some of the causes of crime.	☐	☐	☐
I understand the five aims of punishment.	☐	☐	☐
I know about the effects of imprisonment.	☐	☐	☐
I know how young offenders are treated.	☐	☐	☐
I understand the meaning of parole and early release.	☐	☐	☐
I understand the issues concerning life imprisonment and capital punishment.	☐	☐	☐
I know about community service orders and prison reform.	☐	☐	☐

6 Rich and poor in society

What do I need to know?

- Religious beliefs and teachings concerning individual wealth and poverty.
- The causes of wealth and poverty.
- The possible effects of inheritance, work, indolence, gambling, homelessness and unemployment.
- Attitudes towards the rich and poor in society.
- Issues concerning the minimum wage and 'fat cat' salaries.
- Responsibilities of the state, the community and families in caring for the poor.
- Issues concerning the National Lottery.

The wealthy

People might become rich because of the following reasons.

- Inherited money or property: when a relative or friend dies, as heir to their estate they receive their property. Of the top 1000 wealthiest people in Britain, over a quarter have inherited their riches.

- Earned income: some people receive enormous salaries, for example, top sportsmen or women, top company executives, large company owners, and so on.

- Struck it rich: hundreds of people have become millionaires because they have won the National Lottery or shares they own have shot up in value. Others have created a successful invention and received millions of pounds in royalties. For example, in 2002, Bill Gates of Microsoft was reported to have had a personal fortune of £55 billion.

'Fat cats'

Many companies pay their top executives very large salaries. These are known as 'fat cat' salaries and often include large bonuses if the business is doing well. A survey of 77 companies in the United Kingdom for *The Guardian* in 1999 revealed that the average annual pay of the top executives was nearly £1 million. In addition, many received windfalls from share options, which in some cases amounted to more than £1 million.

Buddhists believe in the Middle Way – a balance between wealth and poverty. Wealth is seen as only a means to an end, not the goal in life. It creates the conditions under which spiritual progress may flourish but just being greedy and hoarding money does not help spiritual development. Attachment to wealth does not bring happiness, but often a person's greed is never satisfied and they crave for more and more possessions.

Some Christians believe that it is God's wish that they become rich (Deuteronomy 8: 18) then some of the money can be used to help others. Others believe that people can become greedy. Paul said that 'the love of

did you know?

A UN Report in 1996 claimed that the top 358 wealthiest people have wealth equal to the combined income of 2.3 billion poor people. That is over 40 per cent of the world's population. It is said that the top three richest people in the world have assets greater than the combined gross national product (GNP) of the least developed countries with their 600 million people.

action point

Companies claim that good managers/ executives work exceptionally hard and their decisions affect the jobs of thousands so they deserve large salaries. Do you agree?

money is the root of all evil' (1 Timothy 6: 10). Jesus taught that loving God is the most important thing and he told a rich young man to give his wealth to the poor and follow him (Mark 10: 25). Jesus warned, 'You cannot serve both God and money.' (Matthew 6: 24)

A Hindu may seek wealth and power, but it must be done in the right way – honestly and lawfully. During the festival of Divali, Hindu businessmen pray to Lakshmi (the goddess of fortune) to ask for her blessings and generosity.

In Islam, it is not acceptable to gain wealth by laziness, cheating, stealing and gambling. Allah creates all wealth and it is His property. Muslims believe that they should be grateful for whatever God has given them and they should use their wealth as Allah suggests. It is wrong to think that you are superior to someone who has less. Wealth and money is only of value for the good it can do.

Jews believe that wealth comes from God but that it is wrong to be too caught up in trying to get rich: 'Be wise enough not to wear yourself out trying to get rich.' (Proverbs 23: 4) A desire for wealth may make a person forget God. The Midrash says: 'He who has a hundred, craves for two hundred.'

In Sikhism, the love of money for its own sake is not encouraged, as one of the five vices is covetousness and greed. Wealth is not that important as it does not last: 'Wealth, youth and flowers are short-lived as guests for four brief days.' (Adi Granth 23) Inheriting wealth is seen as the karmic reward for good deeds in a previous existence.

Poverty

Poverty is not just about shortage of money but is also about having a poor lifestyle. This includes how people are treated and how they regard themselves but at the heart of the problem is the failure to obtain a large enough income.

Some people struggle to obtain the basic necessities for life – food, shelter and clothing. The concise Oxford English Dictionary defines poverty as 'not having the minimum income level to get the necessities of life'. This is **absolute poverty**. There are over 1 billion people in the world who have no access to clean water or an adequate house. Over 500 million people go to bed hungry each night and a similar number of children have no access to school or an education.

In Britain, very few people live in conditions like this but there are those who cannot afford to have electricity, a cooker, a telephone and a television. They live in **relative poverty** when compared to other people in Britain. Statistics show that in the 1990s thirteen to fifteen million people (over twenty per cent of the total population) were living in low income families.

key ideas

Is it not morally right that the rich should help the poor?

Government help

The Beveridge Report led to the foundation of the welfare state in 1945. The idea was to look after everyone 'from the cradle to the grave'. Support given by the government is designed to give everyone a minimum income and includes:

- pensions for the elderly
- job seekers allowance
- housing benefit
- disability living allowance
- sickness, invalid and incapacity benefit
- free school meals
- child benefit.

Some believe that the poor should be required to do unpaid community work in order to obtain their state benefits. They argue that:

- it would give them a sense of dignity and self-worth
- it helps them make a contribution to society
- it discourages people from being lazy and gives them an opportunity to help themselves.

Others argue that this would not be realistic because:

- many poor already have a job that pays low wages
- some are unable to work because they are caring for a member of the family or are handicapped in some way
- they cannot afford transport or cannot get to suitable work.

Minimum wage

The national minimum wage was introduced to protect people from employers paying them very low wages. Those not included are workers under eighteen, apprentices, the self-employed, au pairs and nannies. The minimum wage is a lesser amount if you are aged between eighteen and twenty-one, than if you were aged over twenty-one.

Many businesses opposed the minimum wage. They feared that it would cost jobs, as companies would not be able to pay their employees the minimum wage and still make a profit.

Unemployment

Unemployment is a major cause of poverty. Without a wage many families have to live on state benefits.

Indolence is considered one cause of unemployment. Some people are lazy, show no effort and do not want to work. Without the support of the welfare state, they would be forced to work or go hungry. Some people are not employable because of health problems or lack of educational qualifications or the necessary skills. People over 50 who lose their jobs find it very difficult to find employment. Recent trends include more part-time, insecure and low-paid employment.

Homelessness

There is a real shortage of affordable homes in this country. House prices are out of the reach of many people. Even the cost of renting local authority or housing association housing is not cheap. The result is that thousands are without a home. Voluntary agencies like Crisis, Shelter and the Salvation Army help to provide hostel accommodation.

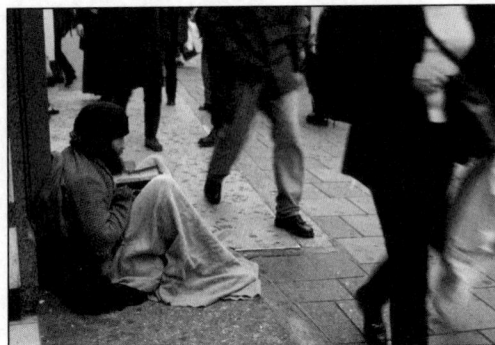

The elderly

Old age pensioners are a section of society who often live on a small income. The State Retirement Pension remains the main source of income for many but this is being seen more and more as inadequate. The Government is encouraging employees to contribute to private schemes as people now live much longer. With a smaller proportion of the total population working, it is becoming more difficult to provide enough money to fund state pensions at a level that would ensure that the elderly are not poor.

Caring for the poor

Who should care for the poor? Thousands are powerless to break out of the poverty trap without help.

- Families: many families are very supportive and help each other, but poverty tends to run in families. Many get into debt by borrowing money, for example, on credit cards.

- Community help: councils, charities and religious organizations give a great deal of help to those in need in their local areas. Sometimes poverty affects the whole community, for example, as the result of the closure of the main source of employment.

- Government help: the welfare system gives assistance to those suffering from poverty and the government has the power to develop national strategies to deal with major problems like inner city, child and rural poverty.

The United Kingdom has:
- 200,000 registered charities

- 200,000 non-charitable voluntary organizations

did you know?

- 400,000 people are homeless in Britain.

- Thousands live in bed-and-breakfast accommodation, on the streets, or in hostels or squats.

- Nearly half a million households live in overcrowded homes.

- Nearly 3 million households live in poor housing conditions.

- 7000 new charities registering each year

- half of the population taking part in some sort of voluntary work

- given over 4 billion hours to charity work

- raised over £12 million in one night for the BBC Children in Need appeal in 2000

- raised over £42 million for the Comic Relief Red Nose Day in 2001.

Gifts freely given bring great merit and the desire to help the poor is important in Buddhist society. Lay Buddhists believe that they have a responsibility to share with the poor. A bhikkhu (monk) is allowed only a minimum of possessions and relies on the Buddhist community to support them. Buddhists should aim between not having enough and wanting too much.

Christians believe they should use their money wisely, as they are accountable to God. The early Christians 'would sell their property and possessions, and distribute the money among all, according to what each one needed' (Acts 2: 45). Jesus taught that riches in heaven are more important than riches on earth and these can be obtained by helping the poor (Matthew 6: 19–21). Many charities, such as Christian Aid, Tear Fund, CAFOD and World Vision, are organized by Christians. Paul taught against laziness: 'Whoever refuses to work is not allowed to eat.' (2 Thessalonians 3: 10)

Hindus believe that merit can be gained by helping the poor. Giving away any surplus is considered a good thing to do, but sacrificial giving is believed to bring unseen merit. Gifts should not be given just to impress people. Many Hindus donate up to ten per cent of their income. This may be used for providing facilities for the community, charity work or the upkeep of temples.

Muslims believe that Allah expects them to be charitable and to help the poor. Being greedy and mean are great evils: 'He who eats and drinks while his brother goes hungry, is not one of us.' (Hadith) One of the Five Pillars involves Muslims giving part of their income as a religious duty (**zakah**). Muslims also make voluntary gifts – **sadaqah**. Muslim charities include Islamic Relief and the Red Crescent.

Jews give a tenth of their income to the poor as **tzedaka** (charity). Collecting boxes are kept in their homes, called **pushkes**. Jewish charities include Jewish Care, United Jewish Communities, the Norwood Orphanages and Jewish hospices. Helping the poor to help themselves so that they may become self-supporting and that their dignity is restored is regarded as highly commendable.

Sikhs are encouraged to help the poor as, 'God's bounty belongs to all, but in this world it is not shared justly' (Adi Granth 1171). Sikhs give at least a tenth (**dasvandh**) of their income to others. This may be given in money, food for the langar, or donations to charity.

The National Lottery (Lotto)

The National Lottery was set up to:

- give people the opportunity to win cash prizes of varying sizes – over 1000 people have become millionaires

- to support good causes.

The first National Lottery draw took place in November 1994. In 1997 it was extended to include a mid-week draw. Some people do not approve of lotteries because it appeals to greed and it encourages people to start gambling. Gambling can become an addiction and people can lose much more money than they can afford.

The lottery has paid over £13 billion to good causes. Money has been given under one of five headings:

- the arts

- national heritage

- charities

- sport

- projects to mark the millennium.

The Buddha taught that selfish desires are one of the root causes of suffering and unhappiness. In this way, gambling on the National Lottery in the hope of winning millions is not an aim approved of by Buddhists. 'Wealth destroys the fool who seeks not the Beyond. Because of greed for wealth the fool destroys himself as if he were his own enemy' (The Dhammapada verse 335).

Many Christians view gambling as a sin because it is addictive and appeals to greed. Some argue that there is little wrong with the National Lottery, particularly as a part of the money goes to good causes.

Many Hindus do not think it is wrong to gamble in moderation or take part in the National Lottery, although gaining money dishonestly will gain a person bad karma.

All lotteries are gambling and haram (not allowed) to Muslims: 'Believers, wine and games of chance, idols and divining arrows, are abominations devised by Satan. Avoid them, so that you may prosper.' (Qur'an, surah 5: 90)

Jews are aware of the addictiveness of gambling and so many urge caution, even in taking part in the National Lottery, but many see nothing wrong in buying a ticket. Some synagogues in the United States obtain some of their income from bingo. It is on days like Hanukkah and Purim that most gambling takes place in the Jewish community.

Sikhs should avoid gambling. Gambling on the National Lottery in the hope of becoming a millionaire is not the Sikh way. Money should be earned honestly. 'A Sikh should live only on his honest earnings. No Sikh should gamble or commit theft' (Rehat Maryada Living according to the Guru's teachings).

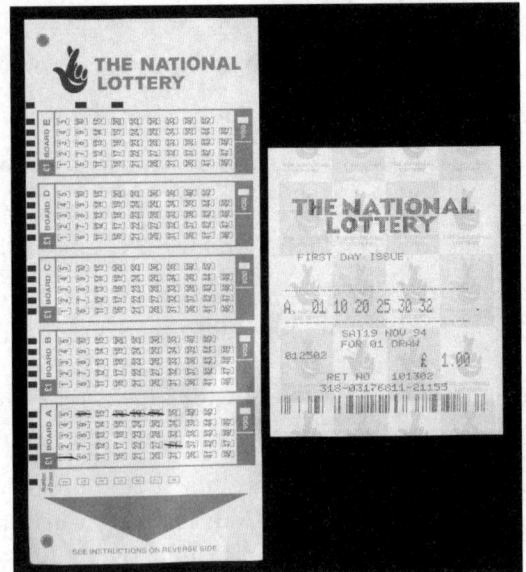

Arguments in favour of the Lottery:

- Over 1500 people have become millionaires since it began
- It benefits many charities and good causes
- Grants are given to preserve religious buildings
- Grants are given which help the community.

Arguments against the Lottery:

- It is gambling and can lead to addiction
- It encourages greed
- The gain is achieved by others' losses
- Those who buy tickets are those who can least afford it
- Any gain depends on chance and is not earned through work or commitment.

Short questions

a What does a 'fat cat' salary mean?   (2 marks)

b What does 'absolute poverty' mean?   (2 marks)

Examination type questions

a Give *two* reasons why people gamble on the National Lottery.   (2 marks)

b 'The poor should not expect handouts.' Do you agree? Give reasons for your answer, showing that you have thought about more than one point of view. Refer to religious arguments in your answer.   (5 marks)

Student's answer

a People hope to win large prizes and become millionaires and if they do not, they are happy that some of their ticket money goes to good causes.

b Some people are lazy and cannot be bothered to work. They get money from the state for just sitting at home, doing nothing. St Paul would say they should not be given handouts but made to work. Muslims have a similar point of view and I agree, but many others are poor through no fault of their own and they need help. Jesus said that we should love our neighbours as we love ourselves. If we were in that situation, we would hope and pray for people to help us. It is morally wrong to let people suffer while we have more than enough. But I do think that it is important to help the poor to help themselves.

Examiner's comments

a Two correct reasons given.   Mark: 2/2

b Basic arguments are given for and against and references are made to religious teachings. Developing the idea in the final sentence to say how the poor might be helped to help themselves would have brought an extra mark, for example by providing the education, skills, equipment or jobs necessary for them to be able to break out of the poverty trap.   Mark: 3/5

Examination practice
Explain the main causes of poverty in Britain. (5 marks)

Checklist for revision

	Understand and know	Need more revision	Do not understand
I know what *two* religious traditions teach about wealth and poverty.	☐	☐	☐
I understand why some people are wealthy.	☐	☐	☐
I understand the main causes of poverty.	☐	☐	☐
I understand what inheritance and indolence mean.	☐	☐	☐
I understand what minimum wage and 'fat cat' salaries mean.	☐	☐	☐
I understand the responsibilities of the state, the community and families towards the poor.	☐	☐	☐
I understand different people's attitudes towards the National Lottery.	☐	☐	☐
I understand what *two* religious traditions teach about gambling.	☐	☐	☐

Glossary

Absolute poverty Not having the minimum income level to get the necessities of life

Abstract reasoning Forming an argument using ideas and thinking the issue through logically

Adi Granth Sacred writings in Sikhism

Bible Holy book of Christianity

Conscience Way of knowing inside yourself that something is right or wrong

Corporate worship Worship performed together

Dasvandh Tenth of income given to charity in Sikhism

Dharma Hindu idea of personal duty or righteousness

Evangelizing Spreading the message of the faith

Evidence Information indicating whether a belief is true or not

Extended families A family that extends beyond the parents and children to include relatives; for example, grandparents

Faith Strong belief in a religion

'Fat cat' A wealthy and powerful businessman or politician

Gene therapy Replacement of a defective cell with a new one

Genetic engineering The procedure for modifying the genetic make-up of cells

Guru Teacher

Holi Five-day festival in Hinduism

Holy books The sacred scriptures and writings of all religions

Human genome Genes that form a 'recipe book' or blueprint for each individual person

Hypothesis Idea used as the starting point for scientific testing

Indolence Laziness

Karuna The idea of compassion in Buddhism

Material dimension The part of life that deals with material posssessions and obtaining things

Mercy killing Another term for 'euthanasia'

Metta Buddhist teaching of loving kindness

Moksha Hindu idea of spiritual liberation

Moral absolutes Ethical statements that are right at all times in all circumstances

Mukti Sikh idea of birth, death and rebirth cycle

Nirvair Being without hatred in Sikhism

Nuclear families Families including both parents and their child(ren)

Palliative care Care given in hospices

Paapa Antisocial behaviour in Hinduism

Pastoral support Help received in personal matters

Piety Religious acts such as worship, pilgrimage or charity

Pushkes Collecting boxes for money in Judaism

Qur'an Holy book of Islam

Reason Use of logical arguments

Relationships How people react and interact with each other

Relative poverty Being poor in comparison to other members living in the same society

Religious communities Groups of people from the same religion

Religious leaders Those in charge or who lead the regular community

Sacred writings Holy books, for example Bible, Qur'an

Sadaqah Voluntary gifts

Samara The cycle of birth, death and rebirth

Sanctity of life The idea that life is special and precious because it is God-given

Sources of authority The place or foundation on which beliefs are based or are obtained, for example holy writings, traditions or religious institutions

Spiritual dimension The part of life that deals with spirit or soul, religious experiences and the search for the meaning of life

Swami Master

Tenakh Jewish scriptures: Torah, Neviim and Ketuvim

Traditions Customs; something that has always been done and is therefore true

Tzedaka Giving to charity in Judaism

Value The standard or principles considered to be valuable or important in life

Viable Used with reference to life, it is the point at which a foetus could survive if it were to be born

Witnessing Acting or speaking on behalf of your faith

Zakah Charitable giving as a religious duty in Islam

Index

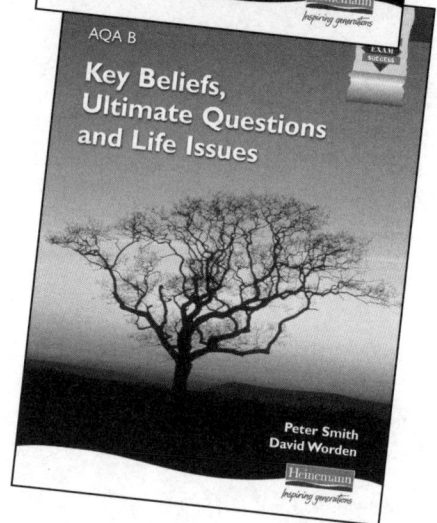